IN
MUDDY
WATER

CONVERSATIONS WITH 11 POETS

ROBERT BUDDE

IN
MUDDY
WATER

CONVERSATIONS
WITH 11
POETS

J. GORDON SHILLINGFORD
PUBLISHING INC

Design and typography by Gallant Design Ltd.
Printed and bound in Canada

We acknowledge the financial assistance of the Manitoba Arts Council and The Canada Council for the Arts for our publishing program.

Thanks to all the poets in this book–indeed it seems indecent to have such pleasure while "working" at increasing poetic literacy. The conversations were not long enough. I do hope this collection expands the number and confidence of poetry readers across the country.

This book is supported financially by the UNBC Office of Research.

"Dennis Cooley: Dreaming His Way into the World" was previously published in *Prairie Fire* 19 (1) Spring 1998: 47-65.

Thanks to Gordon for taking on the project and his care in design.

Finally, thanks to Debbie, Robin, Erin, and Quinlan for supporting such madness.

CANADIAN CATALOGUING IN PUBLICATION DATA

Main entry under title:
Budde, Robert, 1966
    In muddy water: conversations with 11 poets/Robert Budde.

ISBN 0-894283-38-4

1.   Poets, Canadian (English)—20th century—Interviews.
2.   Canadian poetry (English)—20th century—History and cirticism.
I.   Title.

PS815.B77 2003   C811'.5409   C2003-900067-2
PR9199.5.B77 2003

J. Gordon Shillingford Publishing
P.O. Box 86, RPO Corydon Avenue, Winnipeg, MB Canada R3M 3S3

Table of Contents

Robert Budde:

The Interviewer Finds Himself in Muddy Water

RB: So why interviews?

RB: First of all, I like the surprises they offer—you never know quite how an interviewed poet is going to respond. That attracts me, that uncertainty. And I think the poets are also surprised, by my questions and, sometimes, by their responses. I see it in their faces or their syntax. They didn't know they thought that! I like talking about poetry—this is a record of that desire.

RB: What motivates a book of interviews on poetry? What possessed you? What possible role do you see it filling?

RB: I began the project, as you know, in 2000, and it came out of a sudden fear that poetry was dying. This idea made me very sad. More and more of my students seemed to be poetically illiterate and the only way I was finding I could stem that tide was to invite poets into my class to read and chat about their work. Students got turned on by that talk, that "presence," that personality, and the demystification it caused. I thought interviews would approximate those classes and perhaps invent new poetry readers. Pipe dream, I suppose.

RB: Yeah, pretty idealistic. We forgive you though. How did you choose the poets you interviewed?

RB: I know them all. There is no claim to a full representation here and there are far more absences or exclusions than presences. Most of the writers have connections to Winnipeg where I had been located for most of the last decade. I was looking for a range of styles, all which I respect.

RB: Were you looking for contentious issues or conflicts between different types of poetic vision?

RB: Naw. I find it is more an issue of connection. Poetic "conflict" is rarely more than inattention. No, I wasn't looking for dirt. I was after a clear articulation of poetic foundations and principles, senses of history and community. The state of poetry in all its heterogeneity.

RB: Whoa, cool your academic jets there, pal. What is your favourite interview?

RB: See, now, that's just a mean question. Of course I like them all; they each have their own character, their own tenor and pace. Amabile is gentle and meandering, Bruce is raucous and insistent, Kroetsch is evasive and gnomic, McCance is sophisticated and visionary, Cameron is grounded and introspective, Fiorentino is outrageous and cynical, Friesen is contemplative and irreducible, Hunter is fervent and wise, Cooley is playful and generous, Cook is philosophical and precise, Mercredi is reflective and prophetic. I tried to let the interviews unfold in a way that reflected the poets' personalities and rhythms of thought. I was surprised at the different tones each took—I'd imagined they'd be a bit more uniform.

RB: Who's missing?

RB: Well, everyone else, eh. So many, I think a second volume seems inevitable. Certainly, in terms of poetic styles, "language" poetry is a glaring absence. I love L=A=N=G=U=A=G=E poetry but found that there was not much of that going on in Winnipeg; it is more a Toronto, Calgary, Vancouver poetics. I am planning a series of interviews with just langpoets; I am thinking of the title *push* or *xyzed*. Which do you like better?

RB: We'll discuss that later—I want to get back to this project. Why *In Muddy Water*?

RB: Or maybe pushz? I like the look of that.

RB: Yeah. Is *In Muddy Water* a comment on the state of poetry?

RB: *xyzed* can be read in two ways eh: you've got x-y-z with the Canadian pronunciation emphasized or you've got "excised." Or maybe *agnosia*, which means the lack of sensory ability to perceive an object. That'd be referring to the langpo attraction to the non-representational text.

RB: So *In Muddy Water* is more of a muddying the waters?

RB: Poetry has never been more crucial. At this point in history when words are used as powerful political bludgeons, poetry is the only way to take up that language and disarm it. I truly believe it is our only hope. You can stare at it in fear, you can turn away and blindly follow, or you can dive into that completely other way of seeing the world. There is pleasure in sinking, being immersed.

RB: Thanks, Rob. Stay close.

RB: You too.

Catherine Hunter:
A Neighbourhood Poetics

but the streets pull you, they pull you
through them until you are made to understand

"Rush Hour"

RB: I have Catherine Hunter here, author of three books of poetry: *Necessary Crimes*, *Lunar Wake* and, her most recent, *Latent Heat*. My first question has to do with what I think of as your image, as you move through Winnipeg and the Winnipeg writing community. You are seen very much as a "people's poet"; you have a strong sense of working class politics and a vivid apprehension of the everyday. Is that an image you are comfortable with?

CH: I think so. Certainly I would agree that I have a strong sense of community. Absolutely. I grew up here. I have spent my entire life here, although I've lived on the west coast on and off. But, yeah, I feel quite rooted here. I was talking to somebody the other day who moved here from Toronto and I mentioned that someone I knew was hired in Toronto. And he responded by saying, "Boy, these Winnipeg roots are tangled deep." And he was surprised that I knew everyone he had met since coming to Winnipeg. Winnipeg is like that. A number of writers have played off that aspect. Carol Shields is one. There are various neighbourhoods that you become part of, and then the writing community, and the university communities, students, etc. I am not sure what "working class politics" means, but I suspect that it means pretty far on the left and I am firmly there and happy to admit it.

We might as well not exist if we're not going to communicate with each other and help each other out and pay attention to each other. And not just while building things or doing projects but while talking to each other and arguing with each other about how we think things should be done. Keeping all that happening is very important to me.

RB: And that belongs in poetry.

CH: In some ways that is part of the task of poetry. We'd like to think that poetry doesn't try to convince people of things, that it doesn't have a rhetorical agenda, but I think all language does have those things in it. Although sometimes I try to pretend it doesn't. Or I try to hide it, which is just a rhetorical device in itself, eh?

RB: It's very seductive that way. Not in the sense of propaganda but in the sense that you are carrying a message in a very persuasive way—the beauty of it.

CH: I think that most poets would agree that poems that are didactic, that teach and come straight out and tell us "this is the way it is," usually fail.

RB: Because we don't want to be told, we want to see something or discover something. I find in your poems a working-class neighbourhood, filled with people living with each other, filled with clutter and magic and things that you couldn't express in a blunt statement.

CH: No, I couldn't, and I like that description you gave because that's my life. When I'm at home, at least. Often I'm running around, but when I am at home, usually I'm writing, and the neighbours are dropping by or I'm checking the mail and there they are, they're out walking the dog. I walk down my block every day, or I'm in the garden talking over the fence—maybe about the organization concerned about the river that runs by us all, it's called "Save the Seine." The Seine is dirty, it needs to be cleaned again. I take these threads that are around me and weave them into the writing.

> the metaphysical city, her city, with its real
> buildings, its real mess. I want to whisper
> to every invisible thing in the house,
> the way a man once whispered to me
> in the darkness, "don't
> ever leave me. Stay close."

"Mess"

RB: It's like an ecosystem with people interacting.

CH: Yeah, an ecosystem is a great metaphor because everything depends on everything else. We had a terrible death in our neighbourhood this winter, and so many people were affected.

RB: You have a poem called "Opening" with a crazy woman who is important to everyone.

> Finally, the crazy lady moved out
> of the neighbourhood. For years she stalked
> this sidewalk with her fists clenched
> tight as walnuts in the sleeves
> of her unraveled cardigan and talked to birds
> who were not there.

"Opening"

CH: I'll rarely admit this, but that woman really did exist. She did move out of the neighbourhood though, and so the title "Opening" was a kind of a joke meaning she's left and now there is an "opening" for this position of crazy woman. I tried to work with that idea of opening in terms of the theories people had about why she acted the way she did. It seemed to me she was absolutely unrestricted by normal rules of social behaviour. When I went out to get the mail, I really didn't want to see her. I didn't want to deal with her. She'd be walking back and forth down the street. She did actually yell at me one day from way down the street. And I was just crushed because she told it like it was. And now she's gone. I originally wanted to end the poem by saying "no one has replaced her yet. Unless it's me." But the editors thought the poem was too serious to end with a joke.

> Now she's gone and no one has replaced her,
> yet. No one here is qualified to give us
> what she gave us: something breakable and fierce
> we could ignore.

"Opening"

RB: Well, it's nice that readers now have two endings to think of when they read that poem. You talked about the kind of community you have in St. Boniface and it probably would be good to locate you. You're just off Archibald…

CH: The area is called Norwood, near the Seine River.

RB: And then a city-wide writing community you are very much involved in. How is it jumping between those communities?

CH: Most of the time I am quite comfortable jumping around. When I am teaching creative writing I use examples from my own life when I talk about voice. So, I can come in to work today and say, as I just remarked to the department secretary, when I noticed the date was September 29, that this was "the day after the demise of Monsieur Trudeau." Whereas, yesterday I said to my friends, I says, "Hey, I seen Trudeau died, eh?" Very different language, though it's not something you think about or plan, you're not being phony or playing a role. It's just that language is always part of the context of where you are and whoever you are speaking to. I actually have some friends who won't phone me at the university—it's too intimidating for them. Then I will be at my brother's house and forget to put the teabag in the tea and he'll say "Oh, Ms PhD!" People are aware you are moving in different circles.

RB: It's not schizophrenic in that sense, but is it a strain, jumping between those circles and languages?

CH: I don't think it's a source of stress for me. It is for some of the people in my life. Maybe on the odd occasion, when worlds collide, when you're introducing people to each other. Most of the time there's no problem. But once in a while when you're in a social situation... I think women often take on a care-taking role and worry about these things, but most of the time the worries are completely groundless. Everybody's fine.

RB: You talk about your leftist politics. How does that leftist politics fit into an institution like the university? Some people see the university as a place where the left can thrive. Some view it as fairly elitist and class discriminating. Where do you see yourself in the university in those terms?

CH: Wow, that's a huge question. I hope you're not getting me to admit the hidden left-wing agenda in my lectures. [laughter] I have never believed that just because a person is well-educated and wealthy, they are automatically right-wing and politically incorrect. Definitely access to university education should be improved. Though, I believe there are people who aren't suited to the university environment. They are just not interested in the theoretical aspect of things and don't see the point in exploring it.

RB: But if the financial barriers were not there, people who were just not interested would still not come…

CH: But there are people already here who are not interested. They have the money and maybe family pressures, and they want to get a better job. I don't have any solution for that. As a liberal arts institution, we train people to think and explore and question and communicate clearly. We aren't really training people for specific jobs. But they read in the newspaper that people with a university education have a higher income and they come.

RB: We are straying from our initial objective here, so let's dive back into poetry. Let's start with talking about the structure of some of the longer series of poems and what the process is in generating those poems. Specifically if we could address "States of Grace" from *Latent Heat*, "Getting Rid of the Moon," and "Castaway" in *Lunar Wake*.

CH: I'll talk about *Lunar Wake* first, because I wrote those poems earlier. The sequence "Castaway" I would like to say a few words about. The original title of this poem was "13 Poems in Order to Forget You." The poem is an elegy for someone who is dead. Somehow or other, I do not know how, there have been reviews which talk about the poem being about a failed relationship. And, well, yeah, the relationship failed—he died. So, I just wanted to set that straight. The poem starts with the line "reading the book of the dead," and later the speaker says, you have cast my body away, just thrown it away. I suppose if a guy left you, you might say that, but it would be kind of melodramatic, wouldn't you say?

> reading the book of the dead
> no longer understanding language
> the way it promises
> to chase away the seven dogs
> the way it warns
> against the hungry ghosts as if
> you could ward off their yellow light

> "Castaway"

These poems started off with the theme of mourning and they evolved as I wrote them. I started off with the theme of the person left behind, studying the book of the dead, trying to recognize that this life is an illusion and the person's passing is a natural, normal part of existence. But she can't. She can't deal with that. And this is a recurring tension in a lot of my work. A desire to fully have the faith, but the inability to have it.

RB: "Ghost Stories" and your novel pick up on those themes too.

CH: There was supposed to be a kind of irony as these "Castaway" poems progressed, but as I wrote I noticed that what was coming out in the poems were all the little things he left behind: the paint brush, the book he was reading that he never finished, all these little things. I was reading a poem by Osip Mandelstam where Psyche, who represents the soul in Greek mythology, goes to the underworld and Mandelstam says, "the soul is a woman and fond of trifles." And that really hit me emotionally. So the poem started to evolve in a different direction than I had intended to go. It ended up with the title "Castaway" partly because the events mentioned take place on the west coast. But I also used the idea of being thrown away because that's the feeling she has. How could you toss me away like this, leave me behind? So I changed the title because "13 Poems in Order to Forget You" is a humorous, somewhat ironic, title. It no longer fit what was to become "Castaway"—that would have been a terrible title for it. That title had to go somewhere else and eventually ended up as the title of a poem called "13 Lines in Order to Forget You."

RB: Is that a trend—editors editing out humorous stuff?

CH: In that case it was me who decided to change the title. But to answer your question, yes, that is a trend, and I've learned that my humour doesn't always translate onto the page. I can convey it when I read things out loud, making sure that I am controlling the tone of voice, but that doesn't always translate on the page. It is a problem I have as a writer.

RB: I can hear in the lines what you are saying: the way you inflect things, the way you pace things in your reading where the page caters more to the weighty issues because you don't have the control.

CH: Presumably I can achieve a larger measure of that control on the page as I practise and, I hope, become a better writer. But right now I am working on it.

RB: "Getting Rid of the Moon" I've heard you talk about when you introduce it at a reading but maybe you could talk about it for people who have not heard you read. What was the genesis of that sequence?

CH: "Getting Rid of the Moon" turned out to be the title of the first section of *Lunar Wake*, but was my original title for the whole book. There was a particular winter where I was extremely busy with sessional teaching and about five other different jobs. At that time I was just scribbling down lines because I just didn't have time to put them together into finished poems. In an effort to keep myself alive, I did a lot of walking and, I don't know why, but when I talk about those poems I remember a day early in the morning when I was walking to work across the bridge by the St. Boniface Hospital. And there was the moon. The night before I had been writing the getting-rid-of-the-moon poem, and I just laughed because there it was; it was huge, in the morning—it was not going away! The moon to me represents lyricism, romance (and that includes all kind of romantic delusions), lust, and ambition—I guess because man wanted to make it to the moon and did. It also represents poetic ambition, because it is linked to lyricism and romanticism, and the moon is always linked to madness. If you think about it, anyone with any poetic ambition is nuts. The moon represents all those things. I was thinking how one wants to rid oneself of those desires. Even though they can be a lot of fun, they also cause pain. To have love affairs and to have to write poetry, all those things are a pain.

> the moon is a woman (of course) and the man
> in the moon is a transvestite, cloaking himself
> in her silver clothes; or the moon is pregnant
> and the man in the moon is her baby, rocking himself
> in her high gold womb

> "Gender Relations"

I had a notebook that I was writing in during the late '70s on an island off the coast of Vancouver Island. I don't usually save my notebooks, but I had this one, and at one point I was looking through the notebook and looking at the poem fragments and noticed that I had been overusing the image of the moon. I actually had written in the margins, "get this moon outta here!" As a note to myself. I decided not to use that image any more but, of course, it kept creeping back into my work over and over again. I thought, is this some kind of device or trick that poets have…?

RB: Almost like a crutch to fall back on to express feelings and those elements of humanity that language doesn't account for sufficiently.

CH: And so conventional, but it resonates with a lot of meaning, it's multivalent.

RB: So, in the "Getting Rid of the Moon" poems you wanted to pare back the moon image, excise the junk, but also maybe find use in it again.

CH: Exactly. And the fact that it won't go away becomes a joke. Especially if you look at the poems as a whole series. The speaker of the poem gets these grandiose, power-hungry delusions of grandeur and believes she can get rid of the moon. And it always comes back up again. Every night. Just to remind you of who is in control.

RB: "States of Grace" I have been puzzling over and wanted you to talk about how it holds together. These are poems with titles that are all states of mind.

CH: "Delusion," "Blindness," "Nausea," "Hunger"...

RB: Afflictions? Tell me what pulled them together.

CH: It was one of the most amazing experiences I've ever had in my life. And thanks to the Manitoba Arts Council. Seriously. They provided me with a grant which allowed me to stay home, without having to work at all, and write in the summer of 1997. It was absolutely wonderful. I was at that typewriter banging away, banging away, banging away, and it was just a beautiful summer, fabulous. And I was falling in love all over again. My house downstairs is all one room, so I had the front and back doors open so the wind was blowing through the house. And I was gardening off and on. It was like being at the cabin on the lake, honestly, except there's no lake.

I had always wanted to write certain things about my childhood. Not only about my childhood, but about childhood, period. And a sense of family and those things are very hard to write about. I see my creative writing students or other poets at any stage of their careers really struggling with very personal things and knowing that there is some kind of power there but being afraid to release it or let it out. There is a certain confessional aspect to it—you are betraying your whole family, which is something I take quite seriously and didn't want to do. But then I thought, eh, the hell with it. [laughter] I did phone members of my family and ask them if it was okay with them. I think when you're writing you should just go for it, you shouldn't worry about those sorts of things at all. But when you're going to publish, then is the time to worry about them. I do take those things seriously. I have heard some writers say "no, you've got to tell the truth, to hell with the consequences," but I am not like that. I really am not. When it comes time to publish, it is time to worry about it. But I don't think these concerns should stop you from writing in the first place.

Anyway, how those titles and the main title "States of Grace" came to be I am not exactly sure now. All the poems came out in a white heat, over a few weeks, and then I tinkered, tinkered, tinkered. I think the one I was trying to write all along was "Blindness," and I also wanted to talk about the spiritual education that I did or did not get.

> *Why do you take it?* the other kids asked,
> *he can't even see you. Why don't you just*
> *dodge him and take off?* We said nothing
> because back then some things were too powerful to say.
> Our father came out to the doorway, and the kids
> who were willing to risk becoming invisible
> ran right past him and escaped.

"Blindness"

The phrase "states of grace" comes in one of the poems, "Delusion," where she's listening to the minister on the radio, this preacher. My father always hated these evangelical preachers and god help any who came to the door. The missionaries that came around, he just gave them a hard time. And he especially hated the stuff about preachers curing the blind.

In the poem "States of Grace," those "states" include "ignorance" and "fear" and I thought—I often laugh when I am writing, cackling away—I thought it'd be great to have a "state of grace" like "Nausea." Once I had three or four, I realized all the poems I was writing could fit under this structure. And I thought it was funny. When you open up to the table of contents and see states of grace like these, it is obviously ironic. I wanted a way to bring in some irony.

RB: Because most of the poems are cathartic or a sudden realization where you've arrived at some sort of release. Is that fair?

CH: At the end of the series certainly there is a release.

RB: But even in some of the early ones, where you're "drifting over the neighbourhood"?

CH: In this poem, the speaker is "extremely young" and thinks, "it might be possible to drift through life/very easily." But it's not. You are *in* the neighbourhood. We're back to the tangled roots metaphor again. That's ignorance or naivete or youth. She thinks maybe she can get away with it. Sometimes, in other poems, there are visions, there are moments when she realizes things, or thinks she realizes things, but in that first poem she's very naive.

RB: How about the end of "Delirium," again problematic but a kind of arrival at a place of power.

CH: Yeah, and this is nearer to the end of the series. I agree with you that there is a breaking out or deliverance. Even the poem "Hunger," where the young girl is still angry because she feels "I wanted to know where my power had come from and when/it would take me completely." The publisher actually considered that for a title: "Take me completely."

RB: Hmmm. I don't think that works as well.

CH: Yeah, *Latent Heat* is the only title for the book. Anyway, she wants her body to someday crack open so she can escape, she wants that liberation. And there is a previous poem where she dreams that she is—actually I dreamt it, in fact in the poem I don't think it's identified as a dream—a little body inside her larger body scrambling to get out. She knows that if she opens her mouth, the light will come in. But she's pounding on it and it won't open. It was an amazing dream. There's this confinement, constriction, confusion, and then, escape. And she escapes through anger, which interests me.

RB: We don't often validate anger as a way of empowering because it has a stigma, but to see it as a conduit to discovery...

CH: It can be very cleansing. It's an empowering emotion to acknowledge your anger. One shouldn't commit violence, it goes without saying, but when people are screwing you around you *should* be angry, you should be mad at them, otherwise it turns inward and that's where shame comes from, I think. If someone tells you you're a no good kid, it's healthier to say "that adult's a jerk. That pisses me off." But more often than not the kid just internalizes it. And depression comes from that too, I think.

RB: Anything else about the formation of "States of Grace"?

CH: It was probably the hardest thing I've ever written and yet also the most enjoyable. Immensely. I had always complained about the process of writing, that I was tortured. But this...maybe it was because I didn't have to teach at the same time.

RB: You talked briefly about the difficulty in translating the very personal aspects of your life into poetry. Are there examples of this in the earlier books or is *Latent Heat* a breakthrough in that respect?

CH: There are a lot of elegies in my early writing. My friends seemed to be dying with incredible frequency at one stage of my life. So, that's personal, but this is more personal. Partly because my father was still alive when *Latent Heat* came out.

RB: "Blindness" is a heavy one. If I could just shift gears a bit now and talk about lines and line breaks a bit. You seem to form lines partly on principles of breath patterns and a reading voice and partly, occasionally, for an effect, a "semantic turn" you call it, where you have a type of closure at the end of a line but then an unexpected turn at the beginning of the next line that adds a layer of meaning. Is that a fair assessment? Can you talk about your lines in those terms?

CH: You are perceptive there. Not surprising. I would agree. If you were to ask me what are the most common principles by which you break a line I would say those two. I just read a very interesting letter from Andy Patton to George Amabile. This was when I was editing the Amabile issue for *Prairie Fire*. Andy was talking about one of Amabile's poems and he talked about line breaks by saying something like "when you come to the end of the line, the word hangs out there waiting for completion." The ambiguity you talk about is a false sense of closure; it's temporary, an illusion of closure. Andy talks about the rhythm of line breaks as a constant opening and closing, opening and closing, which he describes as the pupil of the eye responding to light. That's a neat, kinetic metaphor of movement. I like that.

RB: I think of a cat's eye, too, as it dilates before it leaps. And there is that anticipation in your line, there's something more, usually there's some sort of turn that contrasts or revises the meaning of the last line. There is that anticipation, that dilation—what's next?

CH: Previously I thought of the line and the turn that can occur as a kind of snaking motion. Meaning is slithering down the page. Or spiraling down the page. I always thought of it as that kind of movement.

When I use line breaks I am trying to control the rhythm to a great extent. You are reading along and then whoop—you're back again. You really have to learn how to read poetry or it would seem like so much wood chopped up in a pile. If you had no knowledge of line breaks, free verse poetry would seem very choppy.

RB: The training also has to do with accepting the doubleness of it. I know students will read along and either want to read the line by itself or will want to ignore the line break altogether and read it like prose. They don't want to have to consider both possibilities. They don't want to integrate both at the same time. They have trouble wrapping themselves around that.

CH: Partly that comes from an approach to poetry that sees the poem as something you have to figure out. It's a secret code. Unfortunately poetry has been taught this way in certain classrooms. To deal with double meanings when you are struggling to unlock the code then becomes impossible. You mentioned "Deliverance" in terms of double meaning.

RB: Yes, though almost any poem could be used as an example.

CH: "Deliverance" is the last poem in "States of Grace" and tells the story of a teenager walking down Langside Street and a guy approaches her and holds a knife to her throat. She becomes angry and that anger becomes a liberating moment for her. Suddenly she sees with absolutely clarity that, yes, she should hate this guy's guts. He's trying to kill her. At the end of the poem, she realizes that "I was the one with the power/I was the one with the knife/to my throat..."

In terms of composition, long before it ever occurred to me to write "States of Grace" in this persona of the young person, those lines came to me. I remember being at The Fyxx coffee shop near Old Market Square, waiting to go in. I was talking with Méira Cook about poetry and there was steam on the window and I wrote those lines in the steam with my finger to show Méira the line breaks. At that time those lines didn't have a place. Sometimes you write things like that down and then later you find out where they belong.

RB: This is exactly the type of ambiguity we are talking about, though. It's "I was the one with the knife/" stop—there's one idea, then "to my throat," then there's another. And then both at once. What happens when the possibilities talk to each other?

CH: To me that's a way of carrying meaning because what I am trying to get across is the contradiction involved. If you have a knife to the throat, you are in the victim position, right? And the other person has the power. So what she is talking about is the other side of it. The victim has a lot of power too. I am not saying run out and be a victim. What I am saying is there is a power that comes from that sort of a situation. In one sense, it's a moral power. And you are furious, if you allow yourself to be. And, like we said, that has a lot of cleansing power. And I am trying to suggest also that there is the power to tell the story, which of course you have to survive to do. This encounter with the knife also made her aware of her own mortality. Ever since you were born you have always been dying. "I had always been dying/to tell these stories." Any idiomatic phrase like "dying to tell stories" or "finish him off"—those phrases are great for double meanings. They have the metaphor right inside them.

RB: I was also thinking of "this generous/forcing open of things"—a "generous/forcing" and that turn across the line.

CH: That seems a paradox. A generous invitation. In some ways it's heavy, heavy irony to say that the guy with the knife on you is doing something generous, but in some ways it was a gift. I am not thanking this guy. If I could catch him I'd kick his head in. I am not saying that I forgive him or that everything in the universe makes sense or anything like that. But seeing as it already did happen, and there's nothing I can do to change that, what do I do with it? He gave me this thing and what am I going to do with it? I wanted to keep turning it and see what might happen.

RB: The idea of autobiography in poetry. You talk about how poems come out of neighbourhoods and family but where does the reader cross the line in assuming this is you? What is the line you draw in terms of autobiography?

CH: Well, I can remember running into this woman who had known my mother and we sat down and she said, "I read your book—now I know your family and you so much better." This was *Necessary Crimes*. Well, I just about went through the roof. It was a terrible experience for a young poet. That wouldn't throw me now—I'd just know that person doesn't really know anything about me from the poems.

The answer I am going to give you is personal just to my own poems. Different writers are going to give different answers on that one. I really do want to convey in my poems what you might want to call "emotional truth." There is a lot of power to it. That's who I am, that's what I am trying to get across. But, as they say in the made-for-TV movies, the names have been changed mostly to protect the innocent. The specific details that you will find in the poems are often lies. I am telling the truth but I am telling it slant, as Emily Dickinson says. I am changing it because I am concerned about certain things coming through. If I am going to write a poem in which I am saying (like in "Gifted," which we might talk about) *why don't you ever follow me? I'm pining away for you and you're not coming around*—I am not going to say who that is! But it's a fairly universal experience, come on, everyone has experienced that in some way. So does it really matter that it was Dick Smith at 56 Ash Street I had a crush on? (I hope there is no guy with that name on Ash!) People who read the poem (and they are out there) and try to guess, *ooh, who is she talking about?* are missing the point. Because the specifics don't really matter.

RB: Yes, these are my emotions but the people, places, and events are not necessarily mine. They are not necessarily "accurate."

CH: And I do use place names and street names occasionally, but in terms of the emotional stuff, I am more careful. I have just as much desire for privacy as anyone else.

RB: What advice do you have for someone who claims they "don't get poetry"? If someone is intimidated or mystified, how do you let them in to your poems?

CH: Good question. How do you read a poem that you don't get? The first thing I would advise is try to get a grasp of the literal meaning of the poem— make sure you've got a good read on the surface, obvious things. Sometimes students will take up a poem and guess at some deep meaning without looking at the surface words. A student will venture, after a long silence, "is it about death?" Look up words, get a sense of the syntax; who is the subject, who is doing what to who, what do the pronouns refer to? That's step one.

RB: That's probably a symptom of the fear, that inability to face language.

CH: The poet wants to let you in. It's not a trick. The other thing I would say is, think of the poem as a voice talking to you. Instead of seeing poetry as some elite or mystifying art form, think of it as someone speaking to you. Think about Michael Ondaatje's "Bearhug"—if someone came up to you and told you a story about his son going to bed, would you be mystified? No. And, after you understand the literal meaning, then you can consider why he might tell this story. What is he trying to communicate? Then you can consider the philosophical questions involved. Does love have a dark side? Even between a father and a son? The poet is trying to open you up to something. It is a matter for discussion.

RB: Instead of thinking there is something locked inside here to pry out, the author is trying to open something up and ask questions.

CH: Yeah, students will begin "I think the poet is trying to say…" The implication there is that the poet is somehow handicapped and can't express himself or herself properly. [laughter] I don't know where these ideas come from.

RB: Part of it is that we are trained to read in a certain way. Openness can be discomforting. Doubleness in language in most circumstances is a weakness. What are you saying? In the poem, that's the richness of it.

CH: And sometimes you just don't connect with a poem. That's understandable.

RB: You mentioned some influences. There's George Amabile and you also did a lot of work on Timothy Findley. He primarily writes novels but how has he influenced your work?

CH: Good question. Reading Findley's work has certainly taught me a lot about voice and about drama. Findley's got a way about him—he's got a lot of guts. Sometimes outrageous. I am a huge fan. Sometimes I'll be reading his books and come to something wild and I'll stop and say, "Oh, come on!" But it works, and why not? It was a liberating experience for me to read Findley and see how he goes out on a limb. I think I picked up a little courage from him.

RB: And what about George Amabile?

CH: George's poetry certainly has had an effect on me. I've learned a lot from his poems and also from him as a person. Here is a guy who is unbelievably erudite. He can talk about poetry and quote lines—he just knows his stuff. You ask him a question on anything and you'll get an answer, you'll get half an hour. He's been a close family friend for over twenty years. To have someone like that in my life has been important. The encouragement he's given me has been almost criminal.

RB: I see a lot of similarities in your poetry—a kind of diction and a deft touch that you both have.

CH: I think we have similar sensibilities. I think that our value systems are very much the same and that may come out as an attitude or as a theme.

RB: The poem "Trying to Say" especially reminds me of a Catherine Hunter poem. The last line brings it down to earth.

CH: Amabile has a recent poem in *Tasting the Dark* called "A Question." The narrator is at a café or bar and philosophizing, and then near the end he phones home and his son asks, "When are you coming home?" He's deflating the whole voice of his own poem in order to bring the reader "home" to a larger truth. It's marvelous.

RB: You write to and for your daughter too. There's a strong but understated feminism that I admire in your work. The way you have your narrator think and speak and move through the world is a stronger feminist statement than, let's say, "feminist theory," because you are engaged with that real world and enacting a strength.

CH: If that's coming out of the poems, I'd be thrilled. And if that's coming across to my daughter, I'd be thrilled. We are so free. It's up to us to create our own lives.

RB: It's partly about learning what freedom is. People have been taught to be a certain person, occupy a certain identity that perhaps is not in their best interest.

CH: But seeing as you are there—what are you going to do now? That's the way I'd like to encourage my daughter to think. You have incredible power and what amazes me is that people are not aware of that power. They really believe themselves constricted when, in fact, they're not. I've lived an unconventional life based on that. And there are people who don't approve, even those close to me who think I should get married or something. And this disapproval probably means I couldn't run for mayor. But my attitude is, so what, it's my life. I am not going to worry about not having a clean house, for example, because someone has told me that's my role. To hell with that. It's my house.

RB: Going back to politics and the personal, Arun Mukherjee talks about "writing back" in terms of power and blame and separately "writing home" as working through identity and issues closer to home. And those two things in concert create the powerful movement or cause.

CH: Yeah, you have to live your life. You only get one. And the older I get, the more I realize how short it is. If there are things you want to do, you have to do them. If I don't work for myself, I am not going to be of any use to someone else. When I write something about the city, and I am describing the city, although it's a lyrical poem, I am hoping to raise awareness at the same time.

Melanie Cameron:
Beyond Wishing, She Wishes

She you he I it they we are
the same thing, words
you shift against each other
as the earth shifts along a fault-line, one
body divided in two, two
bodies moving, we are
moving against ourselves when we move
against each other.

"Between Dream and Open Eyelid"

RB: In your collection *Holding the Dark*, I am interested in the way you shift between the pronoun "she" and "I" (and other places) and then later in "A Spoonful of Rain," "the girl." The poem on page 101 seems to partially address this "split" or dual attention or otherness. By the end there seems to be a collapse, a closing of distance between the identities: "There is no glass between us." Identity is dissolving here in a magical way.

MC: Hmmm. I suppose one could make the case that the book's speakers and many of its subjects— "I," "the girl," some of the "you"s, some of the "she"s, and, in a certain way, "Ophelia" —might almost be aspects of the same persona, viewing and speaking about itself from different perspectives. And the shifting's even more complicated, I think, because sometimes the speaker seems to address an unidentified other, sometimes the reader, and sometimes itself or another aspect of itself. Whooo! Got that?! I didn't consciously sketch the manuscript that way, but when I was reworking the sketches and when I think about it now, that's what I think the book might be doing. And I think you're right that it leads toward the suggestion of a collapse, or closing of distance. Or at least a peace, of sorts, with that.

RB: Knowing you and your poetry, I have been finding myself thinking of the word "mystical." Mystical in the sense that there is a deep wisdom to your poems—they seem to invoke a kind of knowledge beyond knowing. It is a kind of magic you draw on, animating, turning the body, the physical into something holy through incantation:

> The darkness is a handshake.
> Some kind of agreement
> between
> nothing and nothing.
>
> The darkness is that space between
> two open palms, that space inside
> a fist, it is the skin
> around skin.

> "Between Dream and Open Eyelid"

....

> And the mountains are dead, but still
> they know that the earth is warmer, more alive
> than the sun.

> "The Daughters of Silence"

MC: I'm not sure if the poems draw on a kind of magic to animate the body and the physical into something holy. Maybe it's the other way around. I was trying to draw on the body and the physical—the natural things I know—because, through that process, things beyond what I "know" seem to have an avenue to present themselves. Actually, no, I suppose I work at the poems from both sides at once. I often have some "bigger" question I'm trying to solve, or inkling I'm wanting to explore. Those come from a place that feels "beyond knowing." The stuff I sense, but don't quite "get." But then I use concrete images to do that exploration.

RB: I want to circle through two things: the idea of writing out of or into the material world and the idea of accepting the world differently. You described a lot of the poetry as a looking inward, as a restructuring of your perception of the world, how does that relate?

MC: Certain things I perceive will strike me, stand out to me. Simple images usually, or sometimes more complex scenarios. I get a certain feeling—that I have to pay attention and hold onto that thing until I can write about it. Exploring why that thing struck me the way it did, I guess through a process of looking inward, through writing, is a compelling impulse for me. I guess it must be like that for most writers. Accepting and escaping—myself and the world around me—happen in the same instant, in the process of writing. The outside and the inside become the same then, in a way—even through most of the tedious redrafting, because the intense concentration that takes is usually liberating.

RB: If you break down that boundary it becomes a new relationship with the world through poetry.

MC: It's also being in a single moment. I don't know a word for that state or process.

RB: Words like *peace* and *harmony* fit partly because I know you and know there is that calmness, a tranquility around you and I wonder if that isn't part of your poetic journey as well. You talked about being really frustrated with the world at one point in the past. What has changed between that point in your life and now when you seem so at ease?

MC: I'm older, for one thing! I'm kidding, but I guess it's also true that the situations I'm in, specific circumstances in my life, have changed or I've been able to change them, over time, and the way I choose to think about things. I often feel at ease, but there are also lots of times when I don't feel that way, of course! Or at least not on all levels.

RB: There are a lot of love poems in *Holding the Dark* about internal perception and ways in which we as humans make contact, meet in very tentative ways, blend and cross and mix. Is that part of that negotiation of outside and inside? Is that one way the tension is performed? The boundaries are opened?

MC: Some of the poems do begin to explore that. Sure. Relationships, of any kind, with people require our boundaries to open in a way that's much more complex than anything else we open to, I think. Whether it's true or not, with inanimate things, at least in this mainstream culture, we typically feel the boundary is only crossed one way—we take that other thing in. But with people, there's a different kind of tension or struggle. I guess…I mean, I've never really thought this through in quite this way before.

When I lie
    against you
        with my eyes
                closed,
      I bring your body
    with me,
  into the darkness,
      I bring your whole
          body inside
              me.

"Between Dream and Open Eyelid"

RB: You address ways in which we make the self discrete; I break you like a macadamia nut, divide you up. You are someone out there, not inside.

MC: Mhmm. That's how we often think, but is that entirely true?

RB: When you talk about the writing process I've heard you use the word "sketch" quite often. How do you "sketch" out a poem in the early stages? You also talk about establishing a discreet rhythm for each poem—that the poem is driven first by rhythmic tendencies. What is generative about these connections to visual art and music?

MC: Well, I think that poetry is a kind of music. For me, it's not really a metaphor when I talk about rhythms and tones and rests and so on, in poetry. Poetry truly has these properties. I suppose I must gravitate to music and visual art terms, when I talk about writing, because they help me understand and express what I'm doing, or what a poem is doing, in a language that makes what I'm getting at more concrete, more apparent. In a way, poetry is so elusive, in the sense that there are words on the page, but that's not really the poem. That's the score, or the script, or the storyboard. The poem happens in your ear and inside your head. Kind of like the way a dream happens inside your head—it's more than just a thought. Poets, and other "creative" writers, use the dreamscape, or the part of us that understands that space, as canvas, in a way accessing that part of the reader, and painting images there.

RB: The rhythms that you create are subtle; they aren't overstated formal devices like iambic pentameter. Does rhythm generate words or vice versa? How do line breaks direct or oversee the rhythm?

MC: I've been thinking about this question off and on, and I'm not sure that I can completely separate words from their rhythms. Each word has its own rhythm or pulse. And then when you put it beside another word, their rhythms influence one another. After I have a few words together, there's a precedent for how the rhythm can work, and then that rhythmic precedent influences what words will come to me next, or the combination and order they'll come in. But the new words can alter the rhythm, slightly, or add new variations, so long as the underlying rhythm is maintained. I don't know. The rhythms and words generate one another simultaneously, maybe. Every single word has, or partly is, a rhythm, so I really can't distinguish the two.

Line breaks work on at least two levels. They create a brief moment of suspension. The poet can take advantage of that moment to let the line's images sit with the reader, and then can create a cognitive shift in the next line. Get the reader to take in the line, and then change the established image, or speak back to it, by presenting something the reader wasn't expecting or something that enhances the previous line. Line breaks also work to create a rhythmic tension or to support the fluidity of the rhythm, depending on what you do with them.

RB: I want to go back to rhythm once more. I think it is so important to the reading of your poems and it's so important to notice these things—the poem becomes received in a different way. You talked about establishing a rhythm for each poem and so when you are hip-deep in a poem, in the midst of the writing process, and you are writing a line of poetry, how much of your decision making is predicated on rhythm and how much on image or theme or semantic? How much is the next word hinged on sound and harmony and how much on more logic, meaning making orders?

MC: I think they work together. The rhythm becomes a kind of lulling and continues to have the underlying say in what happens. And it's partly by letting myself relax into the rhythm that I turn off my most predictable thinking and clear the way for other images to come to me. Later, when I'm re-sketching, there's more of a balance—I rely on my "rational" mind then, too, a lot. I'll have a line I start with, and it establishes the rhythm. And often I'll start writing with some particular image in mind, too, and I know that I'm going to get to it somewhere, I'm holding onto it, writing toward it. Then other things will come as I write. I'm usually most satisfied with the sketches that come out of that process. Sometimes I begin with a sketch of largely abstract thoughts, and then I build in images and metaphors as I re-sketch, and gradually cut much of the abstraction away. Or once in a while, I begin with a collection of very concrete images and then look for what they are pointing toward, and shape them into a poem. These are the ways I've been working so far.

RB: Can you talk about the different types of poems as produced by these different processes?

MC: Some of the poems I think have a thread that runs through them from beginning to end. Others read more like they've come in little chunks, although I try to shape them so they have their own tensions, or ways of hanging together, too.

RB: A certain number of the poems work off a type of repetition, structured by a repeated line or phrase—are these the kind which typically have that "thread" running through them?

MC: I'll often do that when I'm sketching, regardless of how the poem ends up. When I'm re-sketching, I often cut instances of repetition—it's just too much. Or I might eliminate the repetition altogether. Often a poem doesn't ultimately need the repetition, but I might need it initially to help me maintain the rhythm.

RB: Like a song structured around a chord. Even if the chord is toned down because it was too bold or something, the song is still structured around that base.

MC: Yeah. Or I'm thinking of colour, where one colour attracts others—what draws toward this one colour? At first you might need a lot of that colour, but then you can take a lot of it out.

RB: Or now I am thinking of sketching where you have some bold foundational lines that then establish shape and then you build around those first strokes.

I noticed the word energy came up a lot in your descriptions of your poetry. You talk about the process of writing being quite focused. How do you see energy moving in your work either in the process or the finished product?

MC: Sometimes people talk about intellectual, spiritual, emotional, physical, social energies—for me, in the writing and reading process, all those energies come together. I get to use all of them.

RB: How are your poems physical?

MC: Certainly if I read them out loud there's that physical element—the poems' moving in that way—and of course there's their physical existence on the page. But there's also a blurred physical/non-physical element to poetry. Like I was saying before about dream, as I read someone's poem, the poet creates experiences for me. They happen in my mind, but still somehow also on a sensory level. It's not actually physical, I'm not actually doing what the poem says, but somehow it engages at least the physical imagination, physical memory. This isn't unique to poetry, though, of course.

RB: And it's true, when you are reading a poem, often your body chemistry will change because of what the poem is saying, probably in the writing process too. Anything emotional in writing is translated into the physical. I think ideas, too. We tend to think of our brain as not physical but it's absolutely physical.

MC: Mhmm. By the end of sketching something, I can feel my breathing pattern has changed. I think that's partly because concentrating on one thing like that calms me, and it can be the effect of the content too, but I believe the rhythm hugely influences that for me. The physical and rhythm are so related. We often think of rhythm as something we hear but I think, more than that, it's something we feel. Everything innate, everything basic, is based on rhythm. Labour contractions, walking, breathing, blinking, sex, chewing.

RB: Mother's heartbeat.

MC: Molecules vibrating.

> The girl holds wonder
> in her body, she does
> not let it move
> to her head, it would
> get harder and harder there, like a skull.
>
> Wonder can only preserve
> itself
> in the suppleness
> of skin.

"A Spoonful of Rain"

RB: Aesthetically, would you resist a poetics that pretends to be outside the physical and outside the everyday? Would that be pretentious or self-indulgent or ineffective or uninteresting? Some artists would say that poetry isn't about the world but about the history of poetry.

MC: But what's the history of poetry? Poetry doesn't come out of nowhere and just refer to itself. At the same time, as we're writing, sure we're writing back to poetry. You can't just be a poet in the moment, you are writing as the complete being you are.

RB: Poetry as therapy. Do you think there's a lot to that?

MC: That gets dangerous. For me, certainly it's much more. All of life is therapy, a process. Every day you are learning and reflecting on experiences. You keep evolving. That's a healing, that's living, that's just what we do.

RB: So would you resist a poetics that tries to separate poetic process from any sort of life process—turning it into a game or a puzzle?

MC: Some poetics I am less interested in but, at the same time, I think they are important, and I can appreciate most of them and even benefit from them in some way. Much of the redrafting process is a kind of "gaming" or "puzzling"—trying to get every aspect of the poem, every little piece, to click. I really, really love this stage of writing. But my poems have to be more than just puzzles; they have to have other levels to satisfy me.

RB: If I am teaching poetry and I am breaking down resistance to poetry, I often talk about depth and poems are about having layers which you can explore. This is frightening because it is complex and there's doubt and there's uncertainty about what to focus on and that freedom to move those layers becomes kind of an unnerving freedom for some readers—there's just so much.

MC: Layers, harmonies. I think building a harmony is a bit like a game. To tap out a rhythm is fine but to be able to add a melody and a harmony…

RB: That's where the Yamaha keyboard came in, eh. One of my students asked about lines that are set off from the left margin and she was wondering if readers are meant to pause longer before that line or pause shorter. So, are we meant to "read" that blank space or are we to move more quickly because there is less space between the end of the line and the beginning of the second?

MC: That's a good question. When I use the line that way, at least in the poems I've published so far, rather than creating an aural pause, I'm usually trying to create a syntactic cue for the reader. For instance, I sometimes indent a number of stanzas progressively—I think of that as a "tumbling line," because the images seem to tumble after each other. I'm trying, in those cases, to give the reader a cue that each indented stanza goes back, syntactically, to the previous left-justified stanza. It's a way of trying to help the reader make sense of some of the more convoluted, or extended, sentence structures.

RB: There is a history to the tumbling line or step line that maybe has taught us to read that space differently than other spaces. We don't read back to the margin there. Subtle, isn't it.

MC: Mhmm...

RB: When I used the word "mystical" earlier, it could be that I mean "mythological" because it seems to me you enter the world of myth in a deliberate way; creating new myths out of desire, loss, nature... At least this is one level that the poems work on—re-mythologizing the world. Ophelia as secret, knowledge, fragile, woman, human; Ophelia as artistic field of light and dark—visual resonance; Ophelia as symbolic figure in a mythic drama.

> Ophelia is getting up, leaving
> the soaked heavy dress behind
> like a useless skin, she flies
> naked and free, up from the canvas.

> "Floating Ophelia"

MC: With regard to the conception or "entering" that happens in this book, I've actually done very little in a deliberate way. I knew I wanted to explore themes of darkness—loss of physical sight, the emotions commonly associated with darkness (grief, loss, mourning), darkness as a place of both birth and death, a place of rest, etc., the darkness of one's skin as a symbol that people respond to in a very real way—but that's as deliberate as the thinking was, at the beginning. Of course, the re-sketching, editing and ordering of the book was extremely deliberate. Ophelia, in particular, wasn't a myth to be reworked, in my mind. In fact, I hadn't even read *Hamlet* (shhh, don't tell!) until after the drafting and structuring of the book was nearly complete. And even then, I read it in part because I wanted to plumb the mind of John Everett Millais—the painter of *Ophelia*—not Shakespeare's, the originator of the "Ophelia" myth. I wanted to see what Millais might have been responding to in Shakespeare's portrayal of Ophelia. In a way I didn't understand at the time, Millais's Ophelia represented, for me, a state of waiting, a state of withdrawal from the world, but a state of potential, of gathering or renewing strength. As I wrote about her, I realized I was giving her her senses back, was sort of writing her into a place of rejuvenation.

RB: Your poetics seem both to reflect and depart from the writing sensibilities of your influences, George Amabile, Catherine Hunter, Leonard Cohen—would you call these influences? Talk about how you see a tradition in your writing and maybe a departure from that tradition.

MC: Well, I'd say Dennis Lee's poetry for kids was the first big influence on my poetic sensibility. I used to read the poems in *Alligator Pie* over and over again, as a kid, trying to figure out how he was using rhythm and rhyme and lines. I was fascinated by it. The other original influence wasn't a person, but was the Yamaha electronic organ we had in our house when I was a kid. Yes, this was the '70s! I was taking lessons, learning how to read music and play. And I was moderately interested in that. But I was way more interested in listening to the different beat boxes—"samba," "rhumba," "waltz," and so on. And there was this big green button you could push to get a sort of drum-roll thing that fit the given rhythm! I'd spend hours sitting and lying and hanging upside-down on the organ bench, listening to the different rhythms and switching from one to the next, figuring out what worked together and didn't and why.

Then came Leonard Cohen. The first "adult" poetry I'd read. I was intrigued by the range of his poems—from what seemed like dense political poems, to love poems, slight free verse, poems in rhyming couplets. And I really admired the way he could clinch an ending.

Patrick Friesen was the first "real live poet" influence, in my early twenties. He mentored me, by mail, in the mid-'90s. It was extremely generous of him, and was a tremendously important relationship for me. George Amabile was my thesis advisor and mentor as I was writing *Holding the Dark*. He has also been extremely generous, and has been the most important "hands-on" influence on my writing. Catherine Hunter has been influential as an editor. She was gracious and very helpful in assisting me to fine tune this first book. Sharon Olds, Karen Connelly, Louise Glück. Rilke. Neruda. Anne Michaels… There are lots… They've all been influential in different ways.

But I haven't spent time thinking about how I'd see my writing stemming or departing from a tradition. You could probably argue that it does, somehow, I'm sure, and that would be interesting to hear. But I think it would hinder me as a writer, more than help me, if I were to spend time deliberating over that question myself. That sort of agenda doesn't feel important to me. As I read pretty much anything, I'm studying it to figure out what the author's doing, and I try to use what I learn to strengthen my own writing. And I'd say my writing is influenced as much by other kinds of books and arts and people and things around me as it is by the work of other poets.

RB: What makes you a Winnipeg poet? What in your poetry roots you here?

MC: Certainly in *Holding the Dark* there is a fair amount of Winnipeg, at least a fair amount of the rivers, especially the Assiniboine. I was walking along that river every day I was writing. There's the prairie. But also references to mountains and the North Channel and Manitoulin Island and so on. I didn't grow up in Winnipeg. I moved here in '96.

> To come back from an afternoon
> walk along the Assiniboine,
>
> wash my hair
> with marigold flowers and thyme,
>
> put on a clean white cotton T-shirt,
>
> eat a plum,
> skin the colour of dark wine, flesh
> the colour of grapefruit,
> but sweeter,
>
> to watch the sun fade from the street,
>
> to sit with my sketchbook's blank page
> and a sharpened pencil
>
> "Purple Flowers"

RB: A lot of Winnipeggers are transient so that is not surprising. But what about stylistically, writing devices, do you see yourself doing anything typically Winnipeg?

MC: What would be typically Winnipeg? There's such a huge range of writing here, I don't know what that would be. I know that I've been influenced by Winnipeg writers because I've been able to work with several of them in various contexts, and I tend to read a lot of the poetry that comes out of here. You and I will have discussions about poetry, and your ideas will make me consider new things, but you and I have such different writing styles.

RB: It's an impossible question, I know, but part of it is that answer. I think there's a reason I am calling this *In Muddy Water*. That's a good thing.

MC: Yeah, it's a rich environment. What we share is that we are all familiar with the same scene. Even then it will be a different experience depending on where you live in the city.

RB: Sure, living in St. James or in Wolseley.

MC: Or living here in the North End or Osborne Village where I used to live two years ago—that's a big difference. I look forward to seeing what other writers have said in their interviews.

RB: I know Catherine Hunter writes quite a bit about St. Boniface. You are working on a new book?

MC: Yeah, actually I thought I had a working draft manuscript and was writing new poems for a third book but now I think they might be collapsed together. I'm not sure yet.

RB: Title?

MC: No. Maybe a signal it hasn't found its shape.

RB: Loosely connected poems like *Holding the Dark*?

MC: They seem to be. I'm finding it harder to break into sections than the last book but there is still an inter-connectedness. It has fewer contours, at least at this point. Maybe a sequence without as many defined sections or edges, but…I'm also writing some fiction—experimenting and exploring different voices. Trying to push myself to write something totally different from what I would expect. Someone said that writing one book is not the beginning of being a writer, it's the end of wanting to be one. And I can sort of feel that in myself. I know that I can do this particular thing in these particular ways, but now what else? Other genres, and stretching what I do with poetry. How else can I do it?

RB: Part of the evolution.

MC: Yeah, I guess! Or an attempt at evolution—we'll see!

RB: Despite the first lines ("It happened like this"), this is a book about escape, evasion, imagining a world where images and words and emotions run ("lay my body down, like a river") in a different way, a way you can live with. What do you find intolerable about the world you are revising?

MC: The first line is almost ironic, I think. In a way, the book does sketch out a journey. You begin at one place, and I think you end up somewhere else, by the end. But at the same time, it avoids a narrative structure. It doesn't really tell you how anything happened. It just tells you how things are in select moments. And you have to fill in the gaps between the stops along the way. I'd agree that this book is about escape, evasion, and imagining the world differently, in part. But I'd say that it's at least equally, and maybe ultimately (I'm not sure…I'm just thinking through this consciously for the first time, now), about acceptance and surrender. Maybe it seeks both at once. I guess I don't see myself as revising anything, in this book. I simply wrote my way into and through things that pulled at me. The revision, if there is one, probably happens in myself.

> Beyond wishing, she wishes
> you could feel her, like the poem
> she is. If you could
> feel her that way, she would
> have so many syllables, rhymes,
> a beautiful sound on your tongue, a
> rhythm, you would always know
> where she's moving next, but
> never know just how
> she'd take you
> there. She would
> wrap herself around you,
> like the poem she is. You would rest
> inside her, like breath.

"Purple Flowers"

George Amabile:
Conversations toward "a far point of radiance" and a Tactile Rumination

RB: First of all, thank you for your poems. They have brought great peace, they have incited thought, and they have become a connection between me (passed from tongue to ear to tongue…) and other writers, readers, students, and friends. You have been a mentor, directly or indirectly, to a wide range of writers in Winnipeg, across generations, on and off campus. Tell me about your experience of this influence.

GA: Robert, I've been thinking, perhaps for too long, and I have so much to say it could fill a large book. I can even see the chapters, one after the other with incandescent titles, marching on into the silence of our culture's massive indifference, not only to poetry, but to language itself. I won't write that book, and I will try to restrain my habitual eloquence (verbosity, prolixity). Tonight, I'm a bit worn out, I've been writing and revising poetry all day, but even though I feel a certain lassitude creeping in, I want to begin the process which I hope will prove fruitful or at least productive of a wide-ranging dialogue between us.

My poems were dead things as soon as I finished working with them, and they became, for me, not a living process, but a series of artifacts mummified by typing and printing. Then they were brought to life again, in ways I cannot even imagine, in the minds and lives and conversations and arguments of those you speak of who are the co-creators and the inheritors of that sometimes mysterious process which language makes possible within a community and over a wide stretch of time.

That they have brought peace is a surprise and a delight to me. Though the writing of poems often has that effect on the poet, because of the way it reorganizes and consolidates consciousness, the thought that the same kind of process can occur in and for and through the agency of a re-creative reader is good news. It's what our ideas of writing propose, but because I've not always been convinced by our widely held "reasons for writing," I'm a little surprised and happily reassured by your gracious affirmation that what I've written has been useful to others. That must be the most important kind of validation a writer can have, and perhaps it is even sweeter than the more vivid validation of huge sales and fame.

RB: Can you talk a little about the Winnipeg writing community as it is and was, trends, environments, characters... Who were your mentors and what did they teach you?

GA: The Winnipeg writers' community as it is and was. Well, that's another book. I think the most interesting thing about it for me has been its growth, both in its consciousness of itself, and in the quality of the work it has produced in more and more abundance. When I first joined the English Department at the University of Manitoba, I agreed to speak to the Manitoba Arts Council, as it was then constituted. I don't think it an exaggeration to say I was shocked by the literary climate I encountered there. Most of the members, twenty years or more older than I was then, were generous, civilized, enthusiastic people whose idea of poetry had somehow stalled before the last century had begun. And they had no money to help writers with, nor did they have any idea of how to get it. It was Kenneth Hughes who changed all this, and it is his legacy that we now enjoy, a Manitoba Arts Council that provides significant funding to all the arts, including poets and the publishers of poets.

Myron Turner was important in those early days before Livesay and Arnason and Cooley. He asked me to help him start a magazine, which we called *The Far Point* (from a phrase of Roethke's, who had been his teacher, "a far point of radiance") and the experience, the dedication, the sheer drudging endless labour of that remains for me a testament to the staying power of the small press and its undeniable presence in Can Lit. I met writers who were new to me. Adele Wiseman, whose novel *The Sacrifice* I still find central and reverberating. Jack Ludwig was here for a while, and though Miriam Waddington had already left, she was one of the poets we thought of as part of our writing network. Wong May was here for a year, or a semester, and I remember how hostile she became when I disagreed with her lazy, repetitive lines. Her book, *A Bad Girl's Book of Animals*, had been published by

Harcourt Brace & World (1969). She expected adulation, I guess, but after a while, we were able to agree that we both loved some of the same poets, and I had to admit that there was much in her book I admired.

One of my colleagues at the university was a good friend and staunch proponent of the poet, Kenneth McRobbie, who had published widely and was represented in an anthology called something like *Canadian Poetry* at *Mid Century*. I found his work mostly academic, not that it was moot, but that it was an adaptation of prose discourse, which was also the basic stuff of most American poetry one might find in the more or less established journals then and now. We met occasionally and read to each other, and commented, politely I think, on what we'd heard.

In those days I was the only one who had breached the higher and, as it now seems to me, pointlessly fashionable editorial judgement of magazines such as *Poetry* (Chicago), *Harper's*, and *The New Yorker*. I was even quoted once in a review in *Time*. This was all both good and rotten. Good for the clout it gave me with my students, not that I used it as a club to make them write like I did (though, then as now, how I wrote changed with each poem's lengthy and difficult journey), but as a validation one student described to his disgruntled peer as "All he's saying is that he's been there and if you want to go there too, he can help."

And there was already, I think, though memory is not entirely to be trusted in these, or any, matters of single-minded history, a developing consciousness of the complexity of poetic discourse and its fragmented, though exciting partisans. I remember being introduced by a good friend to the poetry of Doug Barbour, which I did not find exciting. I remember the rapt portrayal of his style, and of many others, as "nothing but the bare bones" and I remember too my response that I was not interested in the poetry of graveyards. I wanted a living poetry, with flesh and blood and tendons and nerve endings and above all a brain that was capable of spritz and incandescence (or something to that effect) and of course there is room for both kinds of poetry and many more. But this was, as I see now, the beginnings of the postmodern distaste for metaphor, elaboration, music, etc. And I guess I just never caught on, then or now, to the direction many wished to drive language in, but I valued, and continue to value, much that the postmodern (though that is a loose and nearly useless term) feels it must discard. I remember a conference at which we argued these things, and I remember saying to someone, maybe Doug Barbour, maybe someone else, who was busting spit in his intense and nearly fanatical espousal of the plain talk theory of writing, the language such as men to speak (Wordsworth, so old, 1800) and I remember saying, sure, why not, but if you want to use the vernacular, if you want to use plain Canadian speech, use it for Chrissake, don't just sleep in it.

RB: And more contemporary connections and specific influences on your writing?

GA: Later, the history is clearer. Cooley. I love his playful intensities now, but then I loved his pure commitments. One night, we drank and argued till dawn, till morning, and found a small ground of enthusiastic agreement, not about particular poets, but about some principles and practices, mostly that any theory is good if it produces good poems, but more than that, we found some poems of Bukowski and Duncan and even that Canadian poet everyone loves and is sometimes bewildered by, who spells words according to his singular muse (I want to leave his name out so you can guess it, it almost rhymes with guessit) we both admired. In the end, it was the energy of the dispute, and the spirit that emerged from it that has sustained, for me, an abiding love, an affection, an admiration for the flavour of his discourse, and the romping self-tripped-up punscapes of his broken lines. More than that. Sometimes, as on page 64 of his new book about his mother's death, Cooley finds a rhythm and a clarity and a cadence that is the real thing forever. And of course there are literally hundreds of writers I could mention, students of mine who are now established, and pecuniary, and almost famous, writers with their own rights and wrongs, but maybe that's not useful here, at least not until you let me know you want me to ransack my raddled backtrack rigorously for this laborious information.

And now the part I like the most. Who has influenced me? Whose being, presence, language, intelligence, wisdom, care and attention has run effortlessly into what I am and what I write. Not the texts but the people. So here they are.

First, and perhaps most distantly, there is my memory of some teachers at Ferris High School in Jersey City and Princeton High School in Princeton, N.J. But even before that. When I was five or six years old, my brother and I and our parents spent a week or two on vacation at Lake Persipenny. We had a little cabin and the place was run by a very old, it seemed to me, and very white-haired ex-teacher named Mrs. Thurston. She once tested my consciousness by playing a game with a dozen glasses. It was a numbers game, I think. And she was very impressed with my mind. More than that, she told my parents, in my presence, that she thought I had a different kind of mind, an artistic way of seeing the patterns. This may have changed my life, but I don't think so. What I remember so clearly was the way her testing was bathed in love. No one who had ever tested me at school had done so in a way that was kind. The idea was, terrify the little shits, and see which ones have the balls (or cunts?) to survive the rigours of scrutiny. Oddly, I did well in those situations at school because I was always capable of drifting into a trance state, much like what we call post trauma shock, and to operate at a distance a few yards above my mortal and physical head. The Thurston experience, however, was exhilarating. After my initial reluctance, her warmth and beautiful voice gave me the courage to let my very quick mind simply do its thing and it surprised the hell out of me (I expected to blow it, and I also didn't care a lot because it would not be on my record, that great threat and eraser of possible knowledge that keeps almost everyone from being able to perform in a kind light) and the sheer fun of having a mind that worked was unforgettable. I still think of her when I don't write well for a day or two, and it helps me remember that it will come, or something workable will come, with patience and focus. I'm not talking about faith in oneself, or that shibboleth the sports commentators beat to death with their small repetitive jargon minds (confidence, she has confidence, her body language exudes confidence), I'm talking about the understanding that mental effort is a simple empty focus that will fill something useful if you let it. Anyway, I love you, Mrs. Thurston. You were in your eighties then and are probably now dead, but not to me.

My father had very few friends. He was, well, dark in his head, as though surrounded by serious brooding of an order inaccessible to children, or even his wife. Still he was not an entire "isolato." The male friend of my father's who came to the house even more rarely than the other few who dropped in once or twice a year was Charlie Renzouli. He was beautiful to look at, long white hair, a big face with large features, a wide smile and strong teeth. He was tall and thick in the chest, wore a black suit, a white shirt, a fat yellow tie, and had big hands that moved when he talked. His voice went up and down and out and back, it seemed to me that he was always about a beat away from actual singing, and he was always smiling. None of my father's other friends seemed happy, except for Will, the tall skinny black man who worked on the railroad, and had six gold teeth. Anyway, Charlie was my favourite. He liked me. He liked everything, and could draw it. Really. Everything. I would name something. Wombat. He would laugh, and in a dozen strokes, there it was on the paper, in the notebook, my notebook that I could keep forever. Or a zebra, a gazelle, a dragon, a mountain goat, a turtle, a herd of buffalo diving over a cliff. This was more than the miracles they talked about at Catholic school. This was physical magic.

And you see, Robert, that your questions are difficult, not because they are arcane, but because to answer them honestly takes a very long time and more words than you could have possibly imagined when you cared enough to want to know what they connect with in a person who has lived for sixty-five years. And worse, a person that old who still has about eighty percent of his photo memory, and can fill in the details ad lib.

Mr. Colinari taught ancient history at Ferris High School. He believed what he knew about them, the Hittites and the endless others, was nearly the same as having lived in their weather. I questioned this. I asked him how he knew. He got annoyed, defensive. Then, one Monday after a long weekend, he gave me a list of books. I read them. We talked. He taught me the difference between what we know about the past and what we think we know. He took my curiosity, my desire to have as much evidence as I could handle, seriously. He told me I had a brain. He told me I should think about becoming a teacher, but not to these rock-and-roll dropouts, to the real students, the serious ones at the university level. I never had the energy, sixteen years later, to let him know how he was right (twenty percent) and wrong as hell about the rest.

Elmore Day. Tall, long-faced, almost like The Joker in Batman movies. Not quite, and very mobile, his voice musical, his style somewhat effeminate. I was never a student in a class he taught. I don't even know what he taught, something not very macho, like home economics, or theatre. Anyway, he took an interest in me. Once we went out at night and drank beer and smoked imported Greek cigarettes down by Lake Carnegie, where the young lovers went to be alone. What we talked about was discontinuous, sporadic, but I remember the tenor and drift of it, how gently he framed what I already knew, that I was clearly one of the front-hall gang, student council, founder and member of the honours committee, but still, apart, still someone who had a distance and a destiny (and here one might sense a probe for some little glimmer in me that might have been gay, I think he was, or if not practising, closeted, and yet what he said was true to my sense of what I had been living for most of my short life) that was different, not vastly different, but not the usual banker's destiny, and the word came out of him with a surprising aura of respect and admiration, artist, he said, "I think you are one of those rare boys [sic] who have a gift, a talent, and if you have the desire, and the vision, you can be one of those we need to show us what we feel dimly but cannot say, cannot see without you." And that was, is, the great half lie I have dedicated my life to. Maybe you have too.

The lie part is the need. One of the arguments for poetry, or any art, I can't really juice with is the one that says they don't know it, but they need us. I believe more than almost anyone in the profound stupidity of most of us and I also believe that stupidity will, in about four hundred years, do us pretty much in, but I don't think poetry, or anything else, can change that by pumping into already stuffed heads, or sucking up to companies for PR money to make poetry a comic book product. Most of my peers talk about writing in a way that will make what we do "accessible" to the "public." And it might work. It has worked before. Diamonds to zircons, and so on. Already the *Globe and Mail* has established its reading level at national standard grade 6. What would it mean to make poetry accessible by taking all the poetry out of it and making it short, short-worded essays or postcard stories that last for only sixteen lines? Do you think that is a reasonable exchange? I don't think any exchange is reasonable. I think the extinction of poetry is reasonable. But I won't pretend it is something else in order to save its memory.

John A. Moore. Full Professor of Classics at Amherst College. He knew them all, Allen Tate, Robert Lowell, Frost, Berryman, Merwyn, the drunks and the visionaries, and he was my first serious mentor because it was then, in those last two years at Amherst College, that the direction of my life was decided, and he was the most important person in my life then, and the direction I took always looked back to him and through him. For two reasons. Because he loved poetry, and because he understood that it could still come alive in a room if someone could say it with love. Even after I left Amherst, we wrote to each other and when I came back from my first teaching here to finish my PhD at the University of Connecticut, I often drove up over the hills to spend a day or a weekend with him, and I felt, though I didn't think of him as my spiritual father, I knew he had something I couldn't find, hadn't been able to find anywhere else. He was a gourmet cook, spare, in the French tradition (I still have a book he used, *Tante Marie's Cookbook*) and we would begin with martinis, have dinner, then move to his back yard and talk in the deepening dusk. Those conversations are a book in themselves, but the one that became the diamond spike, the spine of my later life, was an exchange of words that I've never forgotten. It was late summer, and late in the evening turning toward night. We had been talking about my increasing confusion and doubt about what my life had become, teaching intro English at UConn, and the terrible boredom, the flattening of language I felt as a classroom hack. They don't want to know, I told him, they don't see how it matters, whether they're literate or fucking duck tongued. They really love comic books and they hate Melville. He didn't answer me. We sat for a long time in the deepening silence and the darkening light. "You know, George, you have to trust what you do as a poet to touch and clarify your life as a man."

John Berryman asked me why I wanted to be a poet. I told him some bullshit about helping those who could not speak for themselves and he laughed. Well, he said, and he coughed, you seem to have internalized the party line. But what if not one of those assholes gives a shit, what if they like their own busted language, what if they feel proud of being loyal to those who con and abuse them and rip them off? They think *you're* the fucking enemy because you talk funny. I've read your clumsy derivative *sheiss*, kid. It's not at all bad. Ten years or so you might write something worth a look, but who the hell cares, who'll read it aside from me perhaps and some other poets. You, I asked, totally stunned by all this, you might read it? Yeah, sure, I'm a fucking poet, near a dead one, and not really sturdy, pal, but yeah, me, and maybe a dozen, if you want to be read by some who know what the fuck they're reading. Why don't you take up baseball? Or hey, shoot a movie star. You could sell two or three million without even having to actually to write a single word.

I loved John Berryman because underneath all that true shit, I felt him love me, no, not me exactly, but that thing in me that loved what he loved, the disaster and the tumbling tomorrow of the best that language can do, not for itself, but for its near extinct inventors. This man jumped off a bridge. But he also wrote for decades without publishing, and when he did, he changed the small tight world of the poem.

James Merrill (at Amherst College). He had interesting people come to class to talk with us. Marianne Moore, Howard Nemerov, James Wright, my friend and contemporaries Charles Wright and Harry Strickhausen, Alan Tate, mythical figures like Robert Frost (he was a member of my fraternity at Amherst, Theta Delta Chi, and visited from time to time to give private readings for the brothers), T.S. Eliot (I drove down to Yale to hear his famous speech readmitting the romantics, especially Keats, into his idea of the canon. I was surprised by his size, six foot six at least, and his massive though somewhat lugubrious (Lugosiesque?) voice), Richard Wilbur, and others I'll remember too late.

I read once in one of the Dakotas. It was three in the afternoon. I read well. Afterward, Robert Bly made a point of telling me that he liked my reading. You have this big but sort of quiet voice, an honest voice, the poems are true, and I liked the way they came through me. Later, at dinner, I reminded him that, as the editor of *The Seventies*, he had rejected the same poems I had read. Too bad, he said, maybe they're really crap on the page. We had dinner that evening and he told me three stories about the Zen fool I'd love to tell you here, but maybe I'll save them for my forty-five-page thing on Krishnamurti.

RB: Amazing. All that history filtering into your early writing. Were there then any writing influences here in Winnipeg?

GA: No one here really had much to do with my writing. When Dennis and David asked me to come over to St. John's College I declined, and my reasons were complex. On one level, I wanted to keep the two kinds of writing we represented distinct. On another, I deplored the high school decor and the stultifying offices of St. John's. Also, I interpreted, perhaps wrongly, their invitation as carrying with it a subtle collapse of my poetics, a rapprochement with a praxis I still felt wary of, and which did not satisfy the deepest rough stuff of my ex-American heart. Of course I despise America, so called, what expansive egotism to call a country by the name of a continent it hasn't even begun to conquer. Or perhaps it already owns it, by virtue of the market forces it worships as its national religion. I think it has become our national religion too. Market forces are invoked here too in the way the ancient Greeks invoked Zeus and Poseidon. But they never got their shit together, even the Romans never imagined or named or worshipped a little god of money.

RB: George, tell me more about your perception of "the silence of our culture's massive indifference, not only to poetry, but to language itself"—not that I dispute it, I agree. But what is to be done? What do you say to those who do not participate in any form of language awareness?

GA: I'm not sure anything I said would make the slightest impression. The unified belief that language is natural, like having a nose or a foot, that it is literal and fixed in its meaning, and that it automatically communicates whatever the speaker has in mind is so strong and so immune to evidence or argument based on evidence that there is almost no point in challenging that mindset. Still, I think there are many reasons why language awareness is important even as it is less and less regarded by most people in our culture. Here's one: In a fragmented, nearly granulated society, in which individuals are more and more constrained and driven by ever narrowing definitions of self-interest, language becomes more and more significant because it is one of the few common possessions we still enjoy that might lead to mutual understanding and respect. But even language has become more and more specialized, more and more closed to those outside the group, both in areas of technological jargon and in areas of social interaction in which language acts more as a way of identifying members and excluding non-members than as a medium for complex and nuanced communication between one group and another. The less aware we are of a common language the more difficult it will be for groups with conflicting interests to speak with each other in ways that might make win/win and "outside the box" resolutions possible. On the other hand, given the present indifference to language, a more and more ruthless competitiveness will continue to damage the social fabric and validate more and more violent "solutions" to confrontational disagreements. I think we're seeing a lot of this at every level, from high school shootings which are partly the result of a failure of communication between privileged and bullying student elites and their victims, between children and parents, and between students, school authorities and the community at large; all the way to the dangerous stupidities of foreign policy decisions at the highest levels of power. The abuse of language in political discourse, which almost always degenerates into irrational propaganda, or in commercial advertising, which is misleading at best and blatantly fraudulent most of the time, is a serious condition from which we may never be able to extricate ourselves unless we become more aware of how language works and how it can help to provide creative solutions through intelligent discussion of crucial issues at all levels and in all areas of human interaction. If we can no longer engage each other in richly meaningful dialogue, we may be doomed to more and more violent confrontations and an escalating spiral of destructive behaviour.

I also think language awareness contributes directly and substantially to what we call the "quality of life" (rather than the standard "standard of living," which is nothing more than a bloated consumer index). And of course to be unaware of language is dangerous to one's intellectual health, one's physical health, and one's financial well-being, among other things. So much of what we see, read and hear in public discourse is designed to manipulate nearly every aspect of our behaviour. Our much prized "freedom," to think, and act on what we think, is nothing but cosmetic rhetoric if we are enslaved by our unwillingness or inability to understand the full range of implications in any given text or speech act. To be unaware is to fall victim to the manipulations of political and commercial interests which do not serve us and which, if not checked and opposed, often operate to our detriment. Not participating in any form of language awareness is like not participating in any form of physical exercise. It makes us flabby and less able to defend ourselves, to resist irrational persuasions or to discover new ways of acting in the best common interest. We become isolated, regularized and fall prey too easily to those who use language as a weapon or as a power tool. And power is the issue here, as quality of life is the issue where an absence of language awareness severely handicaps our abilities to communicate, to learn, to enrich our experience and to sensitize ourselves both to what goes on inside us and to what goes on in the outer world. This does not mean that I believe there is no thought without language. Far from it. Intuition and other nonverbal forms of consciousness are a vital part of our lives as sentient beings. But language is crucial to all forms of human transaction, interdependence, cooperation, community, fairness, intelligent decision making, and, ultimately, to our survival as a species, because although we can and do think without language, it is language that makes thought visible. That is a large claim, and I don't have room here to give it the extensive support it deserves, but a shorthand version might begin with the following sentence: Try to imagine humanity without language or with languages that no longer work or work less and less, and see how that immense change in our condition might affect our ability to survive. If we cannot share the experience of others, if we cannot feel their pain and their delight, if we cannot understand the intensity of their convictions, how can we see them as equals, or value them as we value ourselves?

RB: In our last session you brought up "the postmodern distaste for metaphor, elaboration, music, etc." and how you "valued, and continue to value, much that the postmodern (though that is a loose and nearly useless term) feels it must discard." Tell me more about these specific poetic elements you hold dear—what do these contribute to human knowledge that "postmodern" texts do not? Or what aesthetically attracts you to these devices?

GA: I think one of the disappointing things about postmodern poetics, some of them anyway, is their tendency to focus on one element or technique or characteristic of poetry/language/thought and inflate it into a full-blown theory of writing, usually a prescriptive theory, with plenty of "avant garde" rhetoric to forestall serious discussion. Avant PMs are often intolerant of other styles or aesthetics, because they have essentially political motives, that is, to capture the papal seat and establish their own poetic practice (which in my view is often far too easy, too boringly similar to newspaper and advertising copy for instance, and too one-dimensional to have real staying power) as the ruling fashion. And there were arguments about the "vernacular" as well, manifestos that seemed to be saying that the "vernacular" was the only proper linguistic source and model for "real" poems, even though speakers of the vernacular didn't read poetry or care to hear about it. I wondered why the vernacular, and aren't there many vernaculars in any language? Should they be any better as a poetic medium than linguistic sub-categories, such as the street slang of gay male prostitutes, or the technical jargon of chicken pluckers, etc.? And of course the crucial concept in all this blather is use, how does the poet use the medium, whatever it is?

But perhaps I can focus and clarify my contention that postmodern theory and practice often entail a severe reduction of complexity and range of effect by talking briefly about its preference of metonymy over metaphor. Metonymy, as you know, is a figure which names a thing by one of its attributes or by something closely and normally associated with it. This is a figure in which both of the terms (name and thing) are taken from the same contextual field. It is a low-energy, low-risk, low-complexity equation. Metaphor, on the other hand, takes its two terms (older linguistic scholars— philologists?—used to call them vehicle and tenor) from different contextual fields, and the more surprising the conjunction of fields, the higher the energy, complexity and freshness of the figure. This preference for the weaker, less dynamic figure of speech seems to me to be consonant with much PM theory, which argues for things like "accessibility" and "plain speech" and "austerity" and other buzz words, most of which are intended to support a more "democratic" poetic practice but which, in my view, end up supporting just the opposite: the suppression of individuality, discovery, freshness, energy, complexity and depth in favour of a monochromatic, one-voice-fits-all commitment to literal speech and linear thought.

Of course there is no such thing as literal speech. In his remarkable book, *The Poetics of Mind*, Raymond W. Gibbs Jr., Professor of Cognitive Psychology at University of California, Santa Cruz, argues persuasively that figures of speech are not distortions of the literal, but rather essential features of human thought through which "people conceptualize their experience and the external world." I would argue that these figurative aspects of language cannot be selectively excluded from a theory of poetry without also denying an essential technique of consciousness and therefore reducing the range and depth of mental life both in the writer and in the reader. When Robert Creeley writes, in a love poem, "I hate the metaphors," we understand that it is the worn, cliched metaphors of love that he hates, but he doesn't provide us with new ones, and that, in my view, is a significant failure. I think Robert Duncan said the most interesting thing I've read so far about postmodernism. Actually, he was talking about the question of poetic form, and resolved the debate brilliantly by proposing that open form includes closed form. I immediately saw the corollary, that postmodernism includes Modernism as Modernism includes Romanticism, etc. etc.

On the question of aesthetics, the music, movement, cadence, rhythmic balances, syntactic arcs, and other formal considerations are absolutely crucial to poetry (or effective prose for that matter) because they represent and function as the surrogate in language for what we call emotion, that is, they help us to figure forth and to share the balances of thought and feeling, idea and sensation, body and spirit, and so on, those shifting and delicate hybrids without which human experience cannot be effectively written or heard. It is this fullness, this abundance of possibility in language which I miss in much, though not all, postmodernist theory and practice, but even as I speak these words I am distracted by a sense that they are already a little old, that the poetry being written by the very young has already recaptured some if not all of that possibility no matter what theories they may begin with or what new names they find to define their efforts.

RB: Earlier you remarked, "Of course I despise America, so called, what expansive egotism to call a country by the name of a continent it hasn't even begun to conquer. Or perhaps it already owns it, by virtue of the market forces it worships as its national religion. I think it has become our national religion too." I am interested in how "market economy" influences language use and specifically poetry—its production, distribution, consumption, etc. Talk about your uneasy relationship to American writing/culture and also your relationship to sites of resistance to that imperialist domination à la Neruda and other South American writers (or am I mistaken in my hearing them in your writing?).

GA: Perhaps I need a refresher course in language awareness! What I despise is not America, but the betrayal, by a very small power elite, mostly corporate, financial and military, of those values, ideals and first principles which I grew up believing defined the country I loved, but which I realized, in a blinding flash that left me in tears, sitting in a 1949 Ford convertible with the top down at two or three in the morning in a closed gas station in Amherst, Massachusetts, were merely the elements of a cynical rhetoric, a set of carefully orchestrated lies that had no basis in what "America" was, ever, or in what it had become. Freedom, justice, equality, compassion, the sacredness of individual human life, etc. etc., had never actually been real even for the so-called "founding fathers," who preached liberty (for the few) but owned and mistreated black slaves, made fortunes from slave labour and the slave trade, etc., or for that grotesque icon of American mythology, Abe Lincoln, who, far from fighting a(n) (un)civil war to "free the slaves" was himself enslaved by the same industrial interests that bought George W.

Bush the presidency and are lying every day to everyone, through thoroughly owned and controlled public media (the enslaved press) in order to kill half a million people and steal their oil. Lincoln is always presented as the saviour of America's Negroes, but his white supremacist views are almost unknown to even the most highly educated Americans. In a debate with Stephen A. Douglas in Charleston, in 1858, he said, "I am not, nor ever have been in favor of bringing about the social and political equality of the white and black races [applause]—that I am not nor ever have been in favor of making voters or jurors of Negroes." The history of the United States, from the very beginning until this afternoon, has very little to do with democracy (a buzz word, code for state capitalism) and everything to do with power and greed.

On the other hand, it is also true that the United States has a very old and potent tradition of dissent that I admire, as I admire many American writers, artists, actors, musicians. Contemporary poets such as James Scully have consistently resisted the widespread hypocrisy and complicity that has more and more made the phrase "free press" a joke. And yes, I admire Latin American writers such as Neruda enormously, not only for their courage, but for the exquisitely individuated genius of their work. Of course, much of my education and modeling as a poet was based on writers in the British and American traditions. I've named them elsewhere and the list is long. James Merrill was my first creative writing teacher and his generous, articulate, brilliant attention laid the groundwork for much that I have been able to write since taking his class in 1956 or '57. Later, at the University of Minnesota, Howard Nemerov taught me a lot that I didn't want to learn, but which provided a necessary sense of intellectual structure. I still read American poetry and fiction with the greatest interest and feel a deep sense of connection with it, though I have developed much closer ties to Canadian poets over the past twenty years. The books I see lying on my bedside table today are by Patrick Friesen, Patrick Lane, Lorna Crozier, Pat Lowther and Catherine Hunter. The last poetry book I read by an American was *Black Zodiac* by Charles Wright. At various times I've also read avidly (with my stumbling and uncertain grasp of Spanish and Italian) among the pre-World War II Spanish poets and the Italian poets of earlier generations. In translation, modern Greek and French writers have made deep and lasting impressions on my aesthetics and my poetic practice, though these influences are subtle and never easy to detect. And of course the classic translations from China and Japan.

I think the market economy, or "market forces" as they are called now, making them equivalent in most people's minds with climate and the natural laws of the universe, which they certainly are not, affects the "production, distribution, consumption, etc." of poetry in many ways. First of all, because of its control over advertising and therefore of most mass media, it is responsible for the creation and dissemination of a dangerously unrealistic simulacrum—"the generation by models of a real without origin or reality; a hyperreal. Only the allegory of the Empire, perhaps, remains. Because it is with this same imperialism that present-day simulators attempt to make the real, all of the real, coincide with their models of simulation." This simulacrum, which is truth and experience for most people, replaces truth and experience, and so narrowly defines what is acceptable as truth and experience that any intrusion of the real is effectively suppressed, or, worse, recognized as irrelevant and useless. Thus poetry as a commodity all but disappears because it is not part of the simulacrum, the hyperreality which has replaced sensory experience and individual events of consciousness with a reality totally absorbed by questions of consumption and status. The hierarchy of power (and wealth, they are synonymous in our culture) is also the hierarchy of value, of all values conflated into one, and anything that aids or increases that one value is seen as good and is associated with all the other (rhetorical) values (freedom, democracy, justice, compassion, moral clarity, etc.) while anything that resists or inhibits the single, unquestioned value of that hierarchy is evil. You are either with us or against us, you are either good like us or evil like Iraq, which has the oil, our absolute and unquestionable virtue (our single value, wealth, power) requires but won't give it to us. In this kind of discourse, poetry would become incandescent, would burn with the heat of many suns, and must therefore be excluded, or made to seem trivial, a lazy, pointless, unworthy activity, a bizarre and puzzling waste of our time and therefore of our lives which should be spent in serious pursuits that have real results in the simulacrum which is the culture's reality.

Of course, this makes poetry more necessary and important than ever, though it also makes it more difficult to write (because of the devastating impact of the simulacrum on language), more troublesome to distribute (even for free) and almost impossible to sell to anyone.

Duncan Mercredi:

Contrary Wolf in the City

My name is Duncan Mercredi. I come from Grand Rapids, Manitoba. That's where I was born. I am of Cree background, although my dad is what we call a "real" Métis—his mother was Cree and he had a Métis father. My grandfather on my dad's side was a Métis from the St. Norbert settlement before the revolution. That is where I come from, my background. My mother is full-blooded Cree from Nelson House. We are back to being status.

My grandmother was a storyteller. She told traditional stories. In the natural progression in the family, one child is always chosen to carry on the story-telling. By the luck of the draw, or as I consider it, bad luck of the draw, it came to be me. I tell stories using poetry rather than the traditional way of telling stories as my grandmother used to do. My poetry comes from the images and scenes I have seen over the years. Those images are short and sharp. I find it a lot easier to explain where I come from in that fashion.

I worked for the Highways Department for twenty-one years—probably the only native guy working there all that time. Quite an experience to hit some of the small towns in southern Manitoba—an experience I wouldn't want anyone else to have. The guys I worked with were rednecks, but the strange thing was that we became friends.

I don't follow the "Red Path." I am too much of a skeptic for that.

RB: When we talk about poetry, does belief have a lot to do with it? You're questioning a lot of things. I heard you once call yourself a "contrary" person. How do you question faith or faiths?

DM: My grandmother read the Bible in Cree syllabics. Though when someone was sick, she never let the priest into the house. For him to enter meant that they were on their last breath. She sent us off to church but she always said, "take it at face value." To me that meant, priest says something, you leave it there, when you come home, you listen to me. A lot of my writing tries to capture that sense of two fates. It was all right to have them side-by-side but they were not meant to be mixed together. The experience I had with a priest later on illustrated that. What the church was preached, they didn't actually practise. My image of the church was destroyed by that one encounter. One of the new poems I am working on is called "Beef Stew Traditionalists." Because we lost so much in the residential schools and the '60s scoop of the kids, a lot of our traditions were lost. What I call "instant pudding" medicine men came out of the woodwork. They took bits and pieces from different First Nations, groups like the Dakota, the Ojibwe, the Cree, the Dene, and put it all together in a pot, and said, this is our tradition. They're not, because you are mixing everything together. So I have stepped away from the Red Path but also all religion. I am a student of religion— looking for connections, noticing, upholding the differences. A lot of my writing is tied into all of that. I try—I don't think I succeed that often, but I try—to demonstrate how you should treat other people like you expect yourself to be treated.

RB: You use the word "forgotten" a lot in your poems. What has been forgotten? You are questioning, testing that ground of history. What has been reduced, or minimalized, or bled of its power. You mention the Wetigo and the circumstances around your vision of the transformed Wetigo.

DM: Wetigo was to me a being that was there to protect the forests and the creatures of the forest and the bounty of the land. If you were a hunter and took more than you needed, Wetigo was there to take it back. Then Wetigo was used to scare the children. But Wetigo is not evil. Many people nowadays are afraid to talk about Wetigo. I went to workshop of the Aboriginal Writers' Collective a few weeks ago and suggested we write about Wetigo. They said we can't do that. I explained that Wetigo is not an evil spirit and told them the same story my grandmother told me. It made them feel better. They still didn't write about it—I don't think they quite believed me. The young writers still have a block about writing about mythical beings. Because of the church involvement, anything having to do with traditional beliefs was considered pagan. I try to turn it around.

When we were growing up, we used to have a ritual in early fall. The men would go out and hunt as a group and they brought back everything as a group. Then we would get together and set up a camp for both Cree and Métis sides of the river, smoke tents would be set up, we'd cut the meat, hides would be hung up by the elders. All the meat would be shared equally, distributed. From some guy who didn't go out (his portions weren't quite as big, mind you) and to the best hunter. Now, that would cost you. Not like the old days where you actually shared. In springtime when the fish were running, all the men would go the point and haul in the fish, and would be spread around the community again. That's what I learned from my grandmother—keep your eyes on stuff, try to remember everything. Little things like that have been forgotten.

RB: Your Kokum is central to a lot of your writing. Has something been lost in terms of the sexist society we live in, one that doesn't value this kind of wisdom?

DM: There were two old women in Grand Rapids. One of them was my Kokum and another lady we called Kokum too. Whenever anyone needed advice it was those two they went to. And they never did anything without the okay of these two ladies. It was also very rare that a man would beat a wife, because if the community found out he would be ostracized. Once alcohol and white men came everything changed. Once the hydro dam came in, the respect for women seemed to be gone. A lot of times the men went out to hunt, the children stayed back with the women and were raised by them. Because my grandmother and mother were so powerful, I learned that respect and carry it on with my wife and daughters. I am trying to teach my grandson to be the same way. Unfortunately, a lot of that has been lost. The men blew it all, they know nothing, and they blew it all.

RB: In "Kiskisin," the image of your grandmother breathing on the baby is very powerful.

DM: I remember that. Certain times of year, I can still smell my grandmother.

RB: Was sexism a part of an assimilation process by European models and media representations?

DM: Yes. And for me and my community, it came with the dam. When Manitoba Hydro brought in their wives, the men saw that the wives stayed at home and it was the white men that made the decisions. They took that totally, wholeheartedly into their greedy little hands and said we don't have to listen to you women any more. And the change was almost instantaneous. That aspect of our traditions was lost within a year.

RB: A lot of your poems document historical events. What date would Hydro be coming in here?

DM: First explorations were early in the 1940s but they didn't have the technology until the late 1950s to actually build the dam. In 1961 the whole community had changed. It was a totally isolated village before that.

RB: One of the things you said I will never forget. I had you into my class and was talking about paying you and you said, "My writing is a gift, you don't ask payment for a gift."

DM: Going back to my grandmother, because I was the next storyteller I spent a lot of time with her. She raised me until I was twelve and then I was on my own. Once you've been raised by your grandmother you don't have to listen to your parents! One of the things she taught me is that a gift is to be shared. You cannot sell your gift; it's given to you to share. I live my life that way. It drives my family crazy but…

RB: You write poetry and work at…

DM: Department of Indian Affairs. I do research on land claims. Before that, I worked for the province surveying, widening roads, expropriating land to do this work.

RB: Ironic, you taking land for the province, eh?

DM: Ha ha, yeah. I lived in both worlds so I think I have a good understanding, comfortable in either world. I worked with rednecks and had to work harder than them to be accepted. I had a good work ethic based on where I came from. Men getting up in minus forty-degree weather to fish. Now I work in the white-collar world. It's a more alien world to me. You get up in the morning, go to work, go home.

RB: So, you don't feel as comfortable in the white-collar world versus the blue-collar redneck environment?

DM: It's a subtle racism in this world. It's harder to handle. In some ways, I was more comfortable with the obvious redneck racism. In the white-collar world, they'll deny until they are blue in the face. But their actions themselves show you that they are. You walk into the elevator there are still people who will move to the back, very subtle but they move away from you. But they'll still deny they are racist. There is a body language. One of the telltale signs is the phrase, "Some of my best friends are…"

RB: One of the strategies I've taken in my class is to start bluntly arguing that we live in a racist country and we are a predominantly white class and we are racist—I am racist, let's say that, and now what do we do about that, where can we go from that point. Just to get around the denial. That denial won't solve anything. And those subtle racisms are so hard to track, hard to work against. Questions in your poetry get to some of those subtle acts. Walking into a restaurant and being met by silence. A couple of your poems address the idea of belonging. Do you feel at home where you are now?

DM: I feel more at home in Winnipeg than I do back home in Grand Rapids. When I do go home, I want to leave as soon as I can. I don't know why. I feel more accepted in Winnipeg than I do back home. Now whether that's because I've started writing about things I shouldn't be writing about, I don't know. That's probably part of the reason. I've had people come up to me and say, you shouldn't have written this, you shouldn't be talking about this.

RB: What is their reasoning? What are some of the things they are referring to?

DM: Mostly to do with the religion. The abuse. I think the poem "Black Robe" made the people in my hometown very uncomfortable. It actually came out that this priest was doing this. People were unwilling to admit it. It's a good thing this priest is dead now—that's what they said. They're still protecting the priest. Forgot about the kids. Some people now clam right up thinking that if they say something, sooner or later it's going to appear in print. And of course it will—that's what I do. That's why we write, because we want to record our ideas and thoughts. I find that when I work with the groups here in Winnipeg they are more open, like the group that you've got here at the University of Winnipeg. It was enlightening to know there is a white community that is so interested in this writing. At least they were willing to explore our words, our language. That was good. Even in the elementary schools, doing my story-telling, there is a feeling that the kids are listening; they accept what you say. I tell them the story about the mouse at the medicine man's place and to them, it made perfect sense.

This old man used to live down the path from us. He was pretty much ostracized; he had made his own way. He was a traditional believer. He did the tobacco thing when he went hunting. He could talk to animals. A wild horse came into the community and he calmed it down, talked to it, until he could put me and my brother on its back. He lived in this little house that was almost circular. He told my brother and me that there is a little mouse in there that is stealing my food. He would sit me and my brother down on a couch across from the little hole in the wall under the table and set his food out when he went to get wood for the fire. And he gave us little slingshots, just little ones, and always the same amount of seeds, seven seeds. He said, shoot these at him, I don't want you to hurt him; I just don't want him to get my food. And then he'd go out, he'd start chopping his wood and you'd hear him "chop, chop, chop" and that mouse would come out and we'd be playing with it and he'd always eat the seeds and as soon as we ran out of seeds the mouse would run up to the food and take a chunk and then run back in his hole. As soon as that was done, the old man would come back and say, how'd you guys do? And we said, well, we hit it a few times but it still got a chunk of food. He would stick his fingers in his mouth and take out a piece of meat and say, was it like this big? I would go, yeah. How about the seeds? He took the seeds too. He'd say, hold out your hands, and my brother and I would hold out our hands and he'd put the seven seeds in them.

When I ask the kids, who was that mouse, there is no hesitation, no matter where I am at, no matter whether aboriginal kids or white kids, they always say, that old man was the mouse. Then I explain to them about the shape-shifter.

RB: I guess I knew I was going to be a writer one summer when we lived on the farm in Alberta (this was before we moved to Thompson), when I got my first gun. Everyone my age hunted so my dad bought me a .22 for rabbit and prairie chicken. So I got out there and practised with bits of broken flowerpot set on fence posts. Well, this one practice a sparrow flew down and landed on my target, so I quickly shifted my aim and fired. Now, of course I missed but I couldn't help but think, shit, what if I'd hit it!? And I never touched the gun again. At that moment, I knew I was not cut out for hunting and a lot of things that young guys were supposed to be doing.

DM: Same thing with me. I killed a chicken with my slingshot when I was eight. Then my dad got me a gun. Made my first kill with a gun but I felt so bad that I never hunted again after that. The first time was okay with the slingshot—at least the chicken had a chance. It disappointed my dad to a certain extent but he had two other boys who loved hunting.

RB: You talk about your grandmother as a storyteller and you taking that into your poetry. But telling stories to a circle of kids is different from writing on the page, is it not? How does it translate?

DM: It's quite different. The principles of oral storytelling are a lot like Aesop's fables; there is an oral aspect when you are telling of how the skunk got its stripe or Weesigeechak. I knew early on I would be a storyteller but my grandmother said I would probably do it differently. I think she knew I was going to probably be writing. Probably because she saw me reading books all of the time. Once I had a chance to read, I was a voracious reader—everything I could get my hands on. Images and details of my community stuck with me and I knew there was a reason my grandmother always sat with me. She was already training me to observe and remember. She knew that when I decided to write, these images would transfer to paper. I tried to do it in the short story form but it didn't work, it seemed dry—it didn't work the way she had expected it to. Then I tried poetry in high school and it worked. I showed people some pieces both ways, in a short story and in poetry, and they understood the poetry format a lot easier than they did the short story. In the poetry, the idea is there, you can give them the image but there might be an underlayer of meanings.

RB: There is a moral but in a complicated way.

DM: The biggest compliment I have received was from a cousin of mine who read a poem about my grandmother on my mother's side and she was a very gentle woman. She was not a storyteller. She always had a sadness in her eyes. It wasn't until later that I realized she had to give up her kids—when they were four or five they were sent away to residential school. So she lost all three kids in one year and didn't see them again for four years. That's where the sadness in her eyes came from. I wrote a poem about how she was a gentle woman. Then this cousin comes up to me after I read the poem and says to me, how did you get in my head? I hit a chord.

RB: Tell me about the "'60s Scoop." I just ran into this term a few years ago and I don't think many Manitobans know much about it.

DM: The Scoop was the government program in Manitoba when kids were taken from the native communities when they thought the parents couldn't look after them. They would adopt them out of the community. Most of them left the country altogether; some were sent to the States, some overseas. Some horrific stories came out of that, the abuse that they suffered. It was akin to what people suffered in the residential schools. They were just taken right out of the homes. Thousands of kids.

RB: In a few poems, you talk about the idea of a warrior. What do you think a warrior is?

DM: The image of a warrior that we have these days is from Oka or the Manitoba Warriors, the gang. They are just cheap gangsters. The way I see a warrior is as someone who is willing to stand up for their community. You are there not so much to protect the community but you are there to stand as a symbol of what the community could be like: proud, hard-working, truthful, and respectful of other people. At the same time, you are protecting the integrity of your community. Someone who won't back down from their beliefs. You share, you respect, you honour. The warriors you see today are from TV, John Wayne movies, the Hollywood version. If you go back to the old teachings, the warrior was the one who would make sure the community was established in a safe place and they hunted.

RB: Probably the idea of the gang is something that is imported.

DM: Yeah, the saying is that the only "hood" these guys from the res have ever seen is the hood of a car. It's all imported from TV.

RB: Another import could be the blues. What sort of relationship do you have to the blues?

DM: When I was about nineteen, I heard my first Rolling Stones album. I wasn't a Beatles fan. The Stones were rawer, harder edged. I started exploring where the music came from. I researched the history of blues and found this music came from a different world altogether. These blues players and the hardship they went through, the discrimination they went through. I got deeper into it when I moved into the city—I could see the edge, the dirt, the grime, the back alleys. I was attracted to the danger. When you are a young man, these things are attractive. I started to hang around with people who did things that they shouldn't have done. I should have known better too. But it was part of exploring life. It keeps coming back to my grandmother who said that I would do things I wouldn't be proud of. You will survive though. I keep telling people that by all rights I should be dead. I am lucky to be alive. I tell them some of the stories of people I grew up with. Those that ended up in jail, those that died on the street. The blues meshed—I was part of that. Attracted to that sound. It explained where I was going and what I was doing.

RB: Not only that edge, that gritty urban experience but also mourning sadness that I see in your poems. Mourning the losses. Patrick Friesen is also interested in the blues.

DM: Yeah, we did a reading together because of our shared attraction to the blues.

RB: Other influences. You mentioned *Catcher in the Rye*.

DM: *East of Eden*. Edgar Rice Burroughs. Louis L'Amour. I ended up at bush camps and picked up all these westerns. Mysteries. A lot of science fiction. Isaac Asimov—"Childhood's End" is the best story I've read. I started writing when I discovered Maria Campbell. Wow, a native person writing. Before that, the concept just didn't fit. Then it suddenly fit. Then I discovered the beat poets, Kerouac, Ginsberg. Lately, it's been Charles Bukowski. I discovered him a few years back. Drunken bum like him. That's some of them.

RB: And Canadian or local writers? You mentioned Jordan Wheeler.

DM: Yeah, Jordan Wheeler. I am fascinated by many writers. I am always interested to how writers see things differently than me, how they see those streets. Lee Maracle. Jeannette Armstrong. My daughter too really likes her work. My other daughter likes Maracle.

RB: Can't go wrong there.

DM: Then there's the Aboriginal Writers' Collective I am part of: Doug Nepinak, Trevor Greyeyes, Rosanna Deerchild, I enjoy her work, Marvin Francis, I really like his work, Dave McLeod, I really like the way he performs, he is so animated.

RB: Doug has been around for a while.

DM: Yeah, he's drifted away from poetry and is writing plays, which is too bad. Speaking of plays I really like Tomson Highway's plays. Marie Annharte Baker's earlier work I liked. Then she started experimenting in a new genre and she lost me. She's in Vancouver now, I think. There are a few younger writers coming up. I like their work; it's just trying to get them to come out that's the problem. It's hard. It's unfortunate.

RB: This collective will draw them out. The community is growing.

DM: Yeah, the collective is putting together a chapbook, too. It's taking a while because Marvin's working on it. We're going out to Banff together though—we're trying to scrape together enough cash to go.

RB: Pemmican Publications is pretty much an institution here, eh? And you're near finished a new manuscript?

DM: Yeah, actually Greg Young-Ing at Theytus has asked me for it. It would be a different audience. It's a tough call; I don't really want to break away from Pemmican. And a few pieces to go into an anthology edited by Armstrong.

RB: Tell me about wolf and eagle in your poems. Wolf is sometimes associated with the narrator, but sometimes it is obviously not.

DM: I adopted the wolf as my spirit guide. Part of the reason is that the wolf has been marginalized and been made into this evil thing to scare the children. One of my fellow workers told me when his mother wanted to scare them as kids she said that the Indians would come and get you. So, I tie those two together. Plus the wolf has been isolated to little pockets of land where they can live, which is basically what reservations are. The eagle is central to my family. Especially my wife and my children.

Because I was raised in a female society I can identify with both male and female. The first time I read poetry my fellow workers asked me if I was queer. I guess it comes with the territory.

RB: In your books you described Canada in two ways: "awakening" and "having its mask torn off"—can you comment more? Where do you see Canada going in terms of a recognition of itself?

DM: Canada is starting to accept the fact that they are a limb of America. They are part of it. As for "mask torn off," for many years we've denied the fact that we are a racist country and it's been shown that we are. It's surprised them. They are having a tough time living with that. It's become more obvious with the Reform/Alliance Party coming out and saying boldly some of these things. I think you will see a polarity forming, some wanting that American model, some rejecting it.

RB: Describe how I as a teacher here in an academic institution might carry racist perceptions into my classroom and how might I, in my actions, show disrespect to your poems and your ideas?

DM: I don't think there is any way that you could identify that. As with poetry, it's all the perception of the reader. Misinterpretations don't worry me—I am following my vision but know that it won't be the readers' always. That there are instructors like yourself actually bringing this work into the classroom says a lot. There is interest out there. There aren't many native instructors yet that can do this. At least it's out there. If you have questions, come to me.

(Tobacco is given.)

Patrick Friesen:

Taking from the Lord

RB: Mennonite identity (and all the complicated aspects involved) seems less and less a focus in your poetry. Is that correct? If so, is there relief in this? Regret?

PF: Except for specific "projects" like *The Shunning*, I don't focus with very much intention on "Mennonite identity" themes. They just show up, inevitably, I suppose, because of where I've come from. There was a period of a decade or so, where I was quite aware that this is what I tended to write about (simply because my writing, whether poetic or dramatic, songs, etc., is always what is going through my thinking, feeling life at the time). Mennonite themes, undoubtedly, become less overt, more woven into some of the poems. The fact it's less overt is neither a relief nor regret. It simply is. Mennonite themes/issues still weave their way into poems, and often I'm completely unaware of it until the poem is finished, or possibly published. I've just finished a series of "clearing poems," based on two clearings in Manitoba related to my past, and they are settings for meditations, thought processes. It's southeastern Manitoba, Mennonite territory, my physical terrain, etc. So, to what degree are these poems about Mennonite identity? Hard to say. It's always there, one way or another.

RB: *The Shunning* is an early book that is still talked about and taught. What is your relationship to that text now? Your books tend to have a tension between the individual lyric poem and a larger vision or drama. Is it a tension? A generative form?

PF: *The Shunning* is old work. I go years without looking at it. Mostly, it feels quite distant. I can see in my current work that I am still exploring some aspects of language that began around the time of that book. In other ways my language usage is quite different. A lot of important things happened for me in that book, things having to do with form, language, with thought process, old issues, family, etc. It's part of the continuum of all my writing. It's old, but not outdated. Nothing, for me, gets outdated. It's always part of the continuum, and I sometimes find myself revisiting phrases, images, and ideas, coming at them from another slant.

RB: You teach creative writing, so you have a stock of advice and tools to give your students, but what do you depend on getting from your students and other younger writers? Describe what you see in contemporary Canadian poetry trends. How does the Vancouver writing scene differ from the Winnipeg community?

PF: I think what I look for, above all, in my students is adherence to the integrity of their experience resonating through an ongoing working with the English language. Because they are young, they're short on experience in life, and in writing. So, it's a matter of encouraging risk-taking in language, in how they look at themselves, their family, etc. Learning to let go into a freedom of language use and a freedom of interior life. Grab the shelf in the basement where the paint cans are stored and pull it down, letting the paint splash all over the place. Don't be tight-assed about writing, don't be led by theory, don't censor yourself.

I can't say I'm terribly knowledgeable about Canadian poetry trends, or if there are any to take seriously. I have a sense of various groups of writers, busy networking, busy creating "careers," getting the right positions, hopefully winning awards, getting the right reviews from the right people, etc. Still, once in a while I find myself encountering a real voice, a fabric of voice, that feels truthful, that reads like life and death.

The Vancouver scene is more dispersed than the Winnipeg one. For one thing there is a significant difference in populations; this undoubtedly has an effect. There is a sense of community of writers in Winnipeg. In Vancouver, there are various "groups," each with its own poetical/theoretical terrain. To some degree these groupings are age-related/era-related. Not sure if the Winnipeg scene is uniquely "prairie," or what, but there is definitely a greater sense of unity; unity in the sense of mutual support, of knowledge of each other, of frequent interaction. I don't know what it's like today, but aside from some theoretical labellings, I remember Winnipeg writers as all taking part in a basic, single, scene.

RB: Tell me about the "group" you identify with in Vancouver. What figures reside there that create literary energy? How about in Winnipeg—who there were centres of activity?

PF: I don't identify with any particular group in Vancouver. Nor did I feel I was with any particular group in Winnipeg. Not with any consistent theoretical base anyway. Friends, poets with compatible personalities, processes. No schools.

I have only a sketchy notion of what's happening in poetry in Vancouver. It's just a matter of listing names. There have been, and are, many excellent poets, poets of influence, in BC. Names like Tom Wayman, George Bowering, Sharon Thesen, Patrick Lane, Patricia Young, and P.K. Page just touch the surface. I have enormous respect for Page, as a person, and for her work. There are others who made their reputations elsewhere and moved here, poets like Lorna Crozier, Don McKay and Jan Zwicky. There are younger poets, publishers, organizers, making their way up, people like Karen Solie, Wayde Compton, Carla Funk, Ryan Knighton, Brad Cran.

In Manitoba there were numerous significant poets, and literary figures, while I lived there. Going back to the '60s the journals put out by McRobbie, Turner, Amabile. Turner setting up a press as well. Livesay showed up in the '70s, and was important for starting *CVII* and being a force behind the start of Turnstone Press. Of course the St. John crew ran Turnstone. Arnason, Cooley, Lenoski, Beaver, Enright, Tefs later on, and so on. A very important scene set up there. Robert Kroetsch was in and out and part of that.

Other than those mentioned, I think of poets like George Morrissette, Catherine Hunter, Patrick O'Connell, Melanie Cameron, Di Brandt, and others. For me, George Amabile has been, and is, a major literary figure, a poet, editor, teacher, who has had significant influence in Manitoba.

RB: I have situated you as a Winnipeg poet but you are originally from Steinbach, Manitoba. Do you still feel connected to that place?

PF: Yes, absolutely, I feel connected to Steinbach. I think of each place I've lived as a grid that is built within my consciousness/unconsciousness. When I moved from Steinbach, a Winnipeg grid was built on top of the Steinbach grid. When I moved to Vancouver, another grid began building on top of those. So, it means digging a bit to get back to the earlier grid. A kind of archeology of the mind. I find myself moving freely in and out, among, these various grids. They inform each other. Steinbach is an origin. Winnipeg is where I did the bulk of my apprenticeship (which, I feel, is ongoing), of my writing. In a way Steinbach is where I learned most of what I know about what it is to be human in this world, but Winnipeg is where I learned most about writing.

RB: Tell me more about the early stages of your writing career. How did you learn about writing in Winnipeg? Classes? Workshops? Who were your writing teachers (either literally or in spirit)? I am hoping these interviews will give young writers a sense of how they might proceed in their careers.

PF: I didn't attend workshops, courses, in writing. I have ambivalent feelings about such courses (I teach creative writing). If the student understands that a course, a teacher, cannot make him or her a poet, ever, then the course might be useful. It is there to teach craft, to teach a student how to read well. As to the writing, that comes from the individual. If it doesn't, if it's "workshop poetry," it's usually quite obvious. Such poetry is curiously "voiceless." It imitates other voices, and does it well. Great craft, no voice.

I didn't really ever have a mentor, but there were poets I was influenced by at one point or another. Among Canadian poets, Patrick Lane, Michael Ondaatje, Leonard Cohen, Gwendolyn MacEwen, for example. I'm not sure these influences can be spotted, but perhaps. Mostly, my teachers were the writers I read from past eras.

Teachers, like Vic Cowie and Lennie Anderson, encouraged me through the depth of their involvement with literature, excited me about poetry, but they had nothing to do, directly, with my writing.

I wrote early. Usually stories, but often poems. An impulse that I had; perhaps it can be attributed to being immersed in Bible, sermons, hymns, stories and songs my mother sang to me, and whatever reading I did early. I think children understand their world, try to reflect it, explain it, in any number of ways that we, later, call "art." To a child it's just a vehicle. A way of being human in this world. For me, words and music were important very early. It seemed natural to see what I could do with them.

I wasn't very talented in music, but it was probably my first love. I think it shows in my written work. I love to work with rhythm, phrasing, timing; I love the musicality of words.

Probably most importantly, my mother read to me very early, taught me to read before I went to school. She read with me. Writing seemed an inevitable extension of reading. No great decision to make; it was a flow from one into the other. It is to this day. My mother also engaged in some of the discussions I needed to have about living, about the past, about memory. My friend, Ralph Friesen, was fundamental to my intellectual and creative growth in the '60s. Our friendship was a marvelously fertile ground. Endless talks, discussions. He wrote short stories.

I wrote poetry in private because it wasn't particularly "cool" to be writing poetry at the time, not where I lived, where I went to school. I got serious about it in my late teens. By this I mean that I began to write pretty well every day. I learned how to self-edit, how to critique my own work.

At university I spent as much time writing as I did studying. Most of it was pretty bad; my apprenticeship. It never occurred to me, though, that writing was a possible "career." It was something I loved doing; it was in the nature of prayer, often; a way of working things out for myself. More a call than a career.

My university years were wonderful. I loved studying English literature and history and had a handful of excellent professors. I loved the freedom of living on my own in the city, off-campus, writing, reading, wandering about. Personally I knew no writers other than a few of my teachers. I can't think of a better way to become a poet than to read extensively, intensively, and to learn what you can from this reading, from your personal experience as a human.

It's a simple thing to say, but I believe reading widely, and in depth, and living your life as fully as you can, and constantly writing, this is much better preparation for being a poet than a workshop. You'll develop your own voice over time. You'll earn your poetry.

If a person feels the impulse to write, and it becomes something more than over-written diary entries, then that person should simply keep writing. Perhaps a workshop, a course, at some point, might be helpful; but this is not necessarily the best way to go. Read all you can, and write. Writing has to come out of one's life, has to be something integral to one's life. Sooner or later, a person seeks out listeners. With luck, he'll find a good listener, who knows what works, what doesn't, in the poems. But, you don't write to please others first. You do, however, want to communicate in a resonant way; you want to touch the receiving centre of poetry within people.

RB: "Exile" and "loss" are central themes in your work. In *Carrying the Shadow* that "loss" is both expressed and recovered in your representation of mourning and memory after death. Why these attentions? What in poetry allows the expression of these complicated ideas/emotions?

PF: I see my life as an ongoing process of gain and loss, of new experience and memory. Always in the present, pivoting between what I know and remember, and what will be. Exiled in the present, perhaps? Certainly, my personal experience, out of where I came, has a lot to do with loss. Loss which was sought, earned, loss which happened accidentally. Always dealing with loss, and moving on. I think part of what I do as a human being is to remember and honour the dead. I also engage in an ongoing conversation/argument with whatever the hell I might mean by God.

RB: So poetry serves as a type of eulogy or requiem and as a kind of theological intervention/translation? Are both efforts to preserve, trace the past? Gather a place to stand in the present? Writing about loss involves a kind of longing for something—a resurrection, a renewal—what kinds of desire enter into these poems about absence?

PF: Yes, there is writing about loss, but also of gain. Although there is longing for the past, there is longing in the present as well. The human state of longing; something the Spanish understand well in their canto jondo. Basho understood it too in this haiku:

> Even in Kyoto—
> hearing the cuckoo's cry—
> I long for Kyoto.

That human sense of there always being something else beyond the immediate moment/experience, or something behind it, something deeper. The sense that even as one encounters a present moment something is missing.

Poetry does many things, including serve as a fulcrum between past/death and future, through the present living moment of making a poem. Poem as pivot. The poem not in the second base scooping up the ball nor in his throw to first base, but in the moment he pivots from one act to the next.

Not forgetting. A responsibility for the poet. This is different, I think, from "preserving the past." Knowing history is largely made up anyway, the poet's job is to not forget by making resonant chosen details, motions of the past. Eventually, everything is forgotten. It's a delaying effort.

But "not forgetting," I think, gives one ground to stand on in the present. Always coming out of somewhere, something, some people. Recognizing this (a little like Akhmatova's subtle and sly references to her poetic forebears within her poetry).

For me, there's a constant conversation with the dead. Not resurrection, maybe not renewal, just a constant turning back and then back again into the present. A cycle of knowing; taking what I learn from the dead and bringing it back to my present, returning to the dead with what I've made in the present. And so on. Does this make any sense? Desire is very much a part of this. Moving toward, through, absence holds a desire. Partially the desire to fill that absence, perhaps, but more to feel fully the absence and write that absence into the presence of that person or event

RB: I want to trace some more predecessors. Who of the beats influenced you most? How? What has the blues contributed to your poetics? These artistic expressions are normally identified with various oppressed groups (connected to race and sexuality) outside the establishment. Or is being a poet necessarily iconoclastic?

PF: The beats did influence me, but interestingly enough, almost as an extension of the influence of the Bible. Jack Kerouac was the only beat who had an influence, and he had it through his wonderful biblical rhythms in some swatches of *On the Road*. I think I found Kerouac (I read *On the Road* in the late '50s sometime) as a secular continuation of the kind of perceptions, language, rhythms, of the Bible I had been immersed in as a child. I found the long-lined, long-sentence passages suited my own physical voice. I later realized that they were related to certain aspects of jazz. For example, Bill Evans, I find, is a master of long piano lines that I love. So, Bible to jazz in a few easy lessons. A kind of flowing, semi-improvisational, way of creating. This is how I write. By this time I've learned how to edit as I go along, but I try to keep editing minimal till later.

Not sure how much the blues influenced me. I loved the music, but I've only occasionally written out of that kind of tight form. Most recently I co-wrote a blues song with Big Dave McLean. It's amazing what comes out of that kind of compression. I love it. I think, though, the voice I'm most comfortable in, the voice that seems to be part of who I am, is looser, more flowing. What I try to do is keep the compression of the image alive within the flow of my rhythmical approach.

I don't think I listened to, identified, with any kind of music, because it was the sound of oppressed groups. I listened to the music for its own sake. My knowledge of the psychology and sociology followed. Of course, inevitably, elements of the psychological and sociological reality behind the blues, and other forms, would come through directly through the music, not just the lyrics, or the attached stories. I think lieder, canto jondo, fado, and other kinds of music, had an influence on me as deep as blues. Hymns, certainly, had a major influence. Jazz came somewhat later but is ongoing for me. Especially, as I've already suggested, Bill Evans, whether in trio, solo, quintet, whatever. His long-lined playing, his depth of exploration of emotion, of spirit, through sheer improvisational concentration, through his knowledge of classical music, as well as jazz.

I suppose being a poet is somewhat iconoclastic, or used to be. Seems to me it's often part of the wallpaper now. Jockeying for position, competing theories, etc. I don't have much of a sense, out there, of integrity of voice, of experience, felt and thought.

RB: You seem pessimistic about poetry in Canada; it seems filled with competition, "jockeying," "careers," connections. Is it a healthy environment for artistic expression or are there too many community/theory pressures that stilt the writing?

PF: All human endeavours get bogged down in politics and theory, sooner or later. The extent of it comes and goes. Sometimes it's tyrannical, other times it's less obvious. Sometimes it may be necessary to fight it, but mostly it's a waste of energy to think about it too much. What is asked of poets is to be attentive to the world of matter and spirit and to language in the exploration, remembering, and reflection of matter and spirit; what is required is to work and keep working.

RB: What Canadian writers most affected your poetic development?

PF: I think most of my poetic influences are fairly old, and often from other countries. Seventeeth-century English poets like Traherne, Vaughan, Donne, Herbert. Slavic poets like Akhmatova, Tsvetaeva, later Milosz, etc. Rumi, Rilke, Amichai. Canadian poets? I know I like a lot of the work of poets like Patrick Lane, P.K. Page, MacEwen, Ondaatje, Crozier, McKay, Lilburn, and some others. There have probably been some influences here, but I'm not sure what they are, or even if I can spot them. The influences are mostly from outside Canada.

RB: Tell me more about the Slavic poets and how they inform your work. Not many Canadian readers will recognize these names. What poetics do they bring that don't exist in Canadian verse?

PF: What I learn from the Slavic poets is the fully lived life in the face of terror. There is the passion, often eros, in Tsvetaeva; I love the image risks she takes. I love the stately, deeply felt thinking of Akhmatova. I have a sense of how she weaves previous poets into her own work, through subtle quotes, or angles on quotes, showing that she is on a continuum with Pushkin and others. I also understand the impossibly harsh times they lived, and I marvel at their different ways of facing the evil of those years. Poetry was truly a matter of life and death for these poets and, in reading memoirs of concentration camp survivors, I am amazed at the essential value of poetry to most Russians.

Early Milosz sometimes seems too purely intellectual to me, but I love how his wonderful mind has, increasingly, woven heart and intellect together. His books *Provinces* and *Facing the River* contain great poetry.

I once heard Milosz read. He was already in his seventies, but once he stood in front of us, fixed us with his blue eyes, and began to read, I heard the voice of someone young and old; I heard the voice of a poet who, through his determination in Nazi and Soviet times, helped preserve the language of his people, the language of poetry. As with Akhmatova and Tsvetaeva, Milosz writes out of life and death.

RB: Religious imagery populates your poems (like in Di Brandt's, like in Lorna Crozier's). Tell me about the relationship between scripture and your poetics.

PF: I grew up with scriptures, hymns, sermons. My early life was soaked in the rhythms, the phrasing, the resonances, the images, of the Bible. Early on I loved the Bible. It was sheer music to me. When I grew older, and it was taught as dogma, doctrine, I turned away from it. I returned decades later (though, in a way, I never fully left) when I realized that the original music was true, was still there, and I didn't have to bother with doctrine.

It's a complex matter of "not throwing the baby out with the bath water." Working through the scriptures for its music, its resonances, for the spiritual wisdom that exists there. Discarding dogma, wishful thinking, all the self-serving, ideological overlays that have been laid on that book.

RB: I like the distinction between "doctrine" and "music." Is this parallel to the difference between theory or ideology and poetic process? But we live in a world caught up in theory and doctrine—how does one get heard in such a cacophony of conflict?

PF: Yes, comparable oppositions. Seems to me a poet can't get too involved in the ideological obsessions. Just pay attention to what you see in the corner of your eye, what you hear at the periphery.

RB: The "stonelicker" in *carrying the shadow* reminded me of Flannery O'Connor's writing and southern grotesque. What attracts you to the local, the ugly, the gritty, the aching reality of these places?

PF: The local, the detail, that's what matters for me in poetry. I'm utterly fascinated by thinking, thought. Not the finished thought, but the thinking process. Its leaps, its logic, its allusiveness, elusiveness, its echo and resonance. So, "the stonelicker" as a man I watched, as a story I told, as a myth I partly created, partly received, is of great interest to me. When you grow up in a small town, a small community, you see the town drunk, the town fool, the lazy man, the womanizer, the whore, the preacher, the crooked businessman, etc.; they're part of your everyday fabric of experience. They are accepted in a way that some of them wouldn't be accepted in the city, or they'd be more marginalized. They're part of the community. Not hidden away, not institutionalized. The eccentric crosses the street in front of you. You greet him. Perhaps you chat with him, or her. This is the world. The detail, the local. The big generalizations, the ideologies, tend to defeat that real world.

RB: I love this notion—you position poetry as an activity that defeats, or goes beyond, theory, order, the ways in which we categorize or organize the world. Poetry gets at the "incommensurable" (Walter Benjamin) of life—that which is (apparently) extraneous or unrecognized. But why poetry? What can poetry do to represent the thinking process and the "real" that other discourses cannot?

PF: Humans need to measure, catalogue, categorize, and theorize about experience. It's always been done. These last years, those activities have been equated with poetry by some. They are from a different world altogether. Poetry is something else. I think there's big blindness in this with some writers. I believe poetry minimizes this categorizing, ideologizing tendency, knows it's something that can follow the poetic process to help explain it, if necessary; it is, though, not the poetic process itself. Poetry tries to keep experience, and the writing in and through experience, as immediate, as alive, as possible.

RB: Tell me about your take on the "romantic" poet—not in terms of period but in terms of the type of representation. What is your opinion of experimental poetry (whether concrete, sound, "language"...)?

PF: What is "the romantic poet"? I don't know. Bill Evans was often called a romantic pianist. What did this mean? It seemed to mean he was very lyrical, that his work always dealt with the emotional/spiritual life of humans, and that he dug deeply into that life. I suppose it means this is not a pianist, or poet, who experiments for its own sake, most of the time. Experimentation always serves the spiritual, human meaning of a piece of work. Form serves content, and yet form is vitally important. However, ideology of any kind is a dead end, it seems to me.

Experimentation always goes on, and should. Experimentation of form and of meaning. Always, as far as I'm concerned, it needs to serve, help the poet go deeper, farther, always accessible to any intelligent human being who takes the time to read and think. A lot of the language experimentation, variations of deconstruction, for example, I find quite uninteresting and, especially in the beginning, rather obvious. After a while, it seems to me, some writers get so locked into this intellectual game that they end up in labyrinths of writing that seem only barely connected to human experience, human spirituality. Still, one hopes that something useful comes out of some of this writing.

RB: Your line breaks range from a more standard short line to your long wrapped lines (à la Ginsberg?). The wrapped lines appear first in the last two sequences in *Flicker and Hawk*. What happened when you began to write that line? Tell me how you feel out how the line is going to function in a poem.

PF: I think my lines have changed steadily since I began writing. The changes took years to happen. Nothing happened overnight. I wrote conventional average-length lines to begin with. It's what I'd seen, mostly, in books. I studied the meter, the phrasing, in school. I worked with it that way at first. Over time, though (and here public readings were enormously important to me, hearing my own voice, not in my room, but with an audience), I recognized that I wasn't quite speaking in my own "voice," or my voice felt truncated. I didn't pause at line endings. The endings seemed to work on the page, in front of my eyes, but did not work for my ears.

There was no one source for my expanding line. Musical lines helped, Kerouac's long, rhythmical sentences at their best, and prose. Walt Whitman probably played some part in the development of my long line. In *The Shunning*, I worked with the usual poetic lines and with obviously prose lines. I was gradually heading for something in between those two; a long, kind of prosy line with poetic resonance, imagery, rhythm. So, probably it began in *The Shunning*. I wasn't there yet, but that's where I first consciously looked for a line that suited my voice. *Flicker and Hawk* was very important in the development of my line.

I should mention D.H. Lawrence, and his use of parallel structure—his layering, repetition, build-up, from sentence to sentence, within sentences. I haven't gone back to Lawrence in a long time, but I do remember he had a big impact on me in my twenties. I loved how he didn't seem to value words "for their own sake," as individual jewels to be admired, but rather he tried to create lines that actually partook in a motion of being alive. I associate his lines (in his poems as well) with movement, with "aliveness"; words served and were not an end in themselves. There is an immediacy in his work that, I think, probably still stands up where other writers may seem dated.

My poetry opened up utterly for me with the appearance of that long line. I remember *Prairie Fire* (then called something else, I think) first published one of my long-lined poems, and they printed it as an insert in the middle, where you read the long line to the end of the page, without the "wrap." But, I liked the "wrap"; I liked the continuity of that, almost like a kind of caesura at work at the end of the line.

The line is based on a layering of phrases often, a kind of forward-moving repetition that, at its best, builds rhythm, intensity. I very much base the line on how I breathe when I read aloud. The lines, and thus the poems, are about movement. My poetry seems to be about motion, not stasis. I don't work toward the perfect, jewel-like image, or precisely contained thought, or resonance. I love reading that kind of work, but I can't do it. I enter the movement of my thinking process, and of how I then use language. The language use reflects my thought process, as far as I'm concerned. I no longer have to translate my thought process into truncated, precise short lines, with a predetermined meter.

I fully recognize the value, the great possibilities of such writing, but it doesn't serve what I want, and need, to do in my work. I miss something in not using received form well, but I've gained more by heading in another direction. I have my own motion of thinking and expressing. I do, though, frequently work with certain forms I enjoy, within my own lines. I've tried, for example, to work the essence of what haiku seems to me to be within some of my long lines. And, I've tried, fairly frequently, to do the same with the ghazal. There are a few poems that actually, visually, take a ghazal form, but I don't think I've ever written a good ghazal. As with all my writing, I've raided certain forms for what I like most in them, and tried to work that into my own units of breathing and thinking.

RB: I hear William Carlos Williams in your work too—especially the shorter haiku-like pieces (maybe through that Japanese influence). In *carrying the shadow*, there is an energetic play between crisp short-lined image poems and more narrative prose pieces. As one example you have a poem called "the man who licked stones" and earlier you have a prose piece describing the "stonelicker." What different roles do the two forms take?

Most of your books have a cohesive theme or strategy and yet are made up of, almost exclusively page-length pieces. Why does that form of collected fragments (à la *A Broken Bowl*) attract you? Have you been seduced by the long poem (since *The Shunning*)?

PF: I went through a period of reading Williams, but I don't think his influence was that great, or that it shows a lot. I could be mistaken. Whatever is haiku-ish in my work (the actual haikus rarely work as far as I'm concerned, but working in some aspects of how I understand haiku does sometimes work within the longer lines) comes from reading Japanese poets.

I'm always trying to find the best way to write about an experience, a thinking process, person, etc. Some things seem to work only in prose, perhaps fiction, perhaps non-fiction. Some things I've only been able to explore in dramatic form. Mostly, I work with a kind of long-lined, layered poetry that contains elements of story and image. It's about thinking rather than about telling a story. The story is a coincidental part of that motion of thinking. I wanted to do two different things with the stonelicker. I thought I could do it in one piece of work (I also began working him into a drama), but I couldn't. The poem does something complete about him. The narrative does another thing completely. There I needed to tell a narrative around his grave, around his absence in town. Surround the absence to give it a context. By seeing the community around him, what he came out of, by showing the man looking for him, and in the process encountering other dead members of the community, the stonelicker's absence becomes known.

The poem places him directly, as a presence, in the town. Actual memory fused with made-up details, interpretations, helped create a presence.

I have a story, or is it a man, or a role, I've long wanted to write. False starts for over twenty years. I've tried fiction, begun a drama, numerous poems, and I've never felt I was getting anywhere. Perhaps there is another form I need to try. Non-fiction, for example. Perhaps a simple song lyric would catch it best. I've thought of combining forms, as I frequently do, but it hasn't made sense yet. Actually, there are two people like this. Both make discreet appearances in various bits I've written, but neither has found his place yet.

It's possible I've mulled them over too much, thought too much about them. I've killed them off in a way. That's possible. Or, it's not me that should be doing the job. I've brought many others from my past to life, especially in my plays, but these two are holding back. I don't believe just anything can be done. I don't believe you sit down and, necessarily, achieve what you intend. And it doesn't have to do with craft, or skill. Some things are not ready to be written, and perhaps will never be. Some things, perhaps, should never be written. Writing poetry is not separate from living. It's an important thing I do within my living. It interacts with all aspects of my living. There are places of silence that must be respected. There are absences that must remain absent, must be forgotten. I have a lively relationship with the dead as well as the living, a responsibility to them as well as to my writing, my thinking, my remembering. There is power in the well-written poem.

Méira Cook:
Hearsay and Fulmination

RB: Michael Ondaatje calls literature a "communal act." Is it for you? If so, who is part of your community and what is the nature of your interaction?

MC: A community of readers. I never knew who I was writing for; I had no image or person in mind, until I read a wonderful story by Carol Shields called "Invitations" (in *Various Miracles*). In this short story a woman moves to a new address where she finds a careless gift that has been left in her apartment by the previous tenant—a copy of *Mansfield Park*. Throughout that week she receives increasingly beguiling invitations—to gallery openings, cocktail parties, even a formal dinner in her honour. Each invitation is for the same date, the same time, and each invitation fills her with wild anticipation, rash excitement complicated by various fashion considerations: what should she wear? On the Saturday night in question, however, instead of dressing and attending one of her "invitations," she sits down beneath her lamp and begins reading her copy of *Mansfield Park*, soon losing herself in the pages. All the people hurrying by her window, distracted by invitations of their own, glance in on this reading woman glowing beneath the rays of her lamp:

> Those who passed by and saw her were seized by a twist of pain, which was really a kind of nostalgia for their childhood and for a simplified time when they, too, had been bonded to the books they read and to certain golden rooms which they remembered as being complete and perfect as stage settings.
>
> Carol Shields, "Invitations"

When I read this beautiful story (which I hope I've not spoiled by paraphrasing in this way) I knew exactly who I was writing for: the woman who ignores all her invitations in order to stay home and read; the passersby who envy her solitude and the light falling in bright astonishment upon her page.

RB: You often entertain fable, legend, myth or fairy-tale in your poetry. Why that intertextual attention? What draws you to re-articulate these narratives?

MC: Perhaps there is a hunger in these stories that I remember from childhood. Or a hunger, at least, in my memory of childhood reading. Remember the "twist of pain" the passersby in the Shields short story experienced that was also a nostalgia for that simplified time in which they were able to lose themselves in their golden books and the world faded away entirely, irretrievably?

Hunger. I often think about those poor children, Hansel and Gretel, the saddest fairy-tale in the world, perhaps. What would convince a mother to lose her children in the woods? Well, the family was in danger of starving, you see, she was hungry. And the children were hungry also and perhaps she anticipated a house made of gingerbread and frosting somewhere in their future. But when we read this story, at least when I do, it's not the handfuls of cake and shoveled wine gums I remember, not even the little boy slowly fattening like a goose in his cage, but the wild hunger that must have stalked that starving mother as she led her children deeper and deeper into the woods.

To me this is the hunger of reading. Perhaps the next book we read will explain why the mother did what she did which is, after all, inconceivable. And if not this one then the next.

There is a story, perhaps a fairy-tale or a myth but a story nonetheless, that a religious Jew teaches her child the value of learning, of reading, by spreading honey on the page. As sweet as the honey so is reading; that is the lesson. But what this story—as lovely, as symbolic and full-throated as it is— obscures is the hunger that exists before the honey, the hunger that makes little children want to eat up their books.

I recently attended a lecture by Anne Carson, a wonderful poet; she was talking about religious devotion, female mystics who starved themselves for love of God. At the end, she speculated about this audacious connection between food and adoration and this led to her own memories of early reading. She recalled a book she was given as a child, a *Lives of the Saints*.

The pictures were so beautiful, the writing so colourful, that it was all she could do—indeed, she succumbed to appetite, in the end, and her parents had to take the book from her—all she could do not to put her mouth to the golden halos and rosy cheeks of the blessed saints, their devout, upturned eyes and Eat Them Up.

There is a hunger in reading. And the more we read the hungrier we become.

RB: I've named a type of metaphor after you (the Cookesque Prepositional Metaphor) in which you swing a metaphor around a preposition. Why are you attracted to that shape of trope?

MC: It's very sweet of you to inaugurate the Cookesque Prepositional Metaphor, Rob, and also dastardly cunning because now I'm effectively banned from using such a trope, of course. Ever again. But you're quite correct about the insidious effect that metaphors have had on me; metaphors in particular and language, or rather the experience of falling into language, in general.

In fact, I remember my first metaphor perfectly. It happened somewhere between learning to speak and learning to read. I was old enough to love stories but too young to read them for myself and every night my father would take down Andrew Lang's *Crimson Fairy Book* and turn to the story of *The Little Mermaid*, which was always my first request. It was after the mermaid falls in love with the prince, after she sells her voice to the sea-witch to gain the legs she requires to pursue him. You remember, she is washed ashore in view of the castle, the prince who is walking on the beach sees a fallen woman and rushes down to save her as princes are inclined to do. She starts awake, scrambles to her feet and stumbles toward him—and now listen—"each step was like knives." *Each step was like knives*, my father's voice repeated, *each step was like knives* and I was suddenly, gradually, all at once, or little by little thrown open to comparison, to the lying word, to the spaces between stairs and to the sudden gashes in the world that words strike, here and here.

It was during this story, during this sentence, that I first became aware of words not as objects in the world, clunky blocks with which to build sentences, but as little hinges that let you into and out of ideas. It was during this story, this sentence that narrative suddenly gaped into language for me as if a glossy six by four photograph had been enlarged beyond recognition of anything but the grain beneath. Do you see how one metaphor leads to another?

As soon as I heard those words, "each step was like knives," I was inaugurated into a world of inexact correspondences, where words not only stood for emotions (knife for pain) but replaced them. Where the mermaid stood agonized and love-struck upon the sand, a knife began to grow from her heel, the hilt digging in. Perhaps my own ankles began to ache a little, perhaps I felt the serrations at the surface of my skin, the shaft of a blade lodged deep within my Achilles tendon. (Or perhaps I was too young and felt nothing of the sort, perhaps I fell asleep soon after and my father gently pulled the blanket over my shoulder before shutting the book.) But I cannot read those words today without feeling my legs give way *like knives*, without feeling my body succumb to language and its covert alliances.

Jacques Lacan, who has theorized these alliances at some length, characterizes the metaphor as a subtle flare of meaning, a discrete conflagration on the page:

> The creative spark of the metaphor does not spring from the presentation of two images, that is, of two signifiers equally actualized. It flashes between two signifiers, one of which has taken the place of the other in the signifying chain, the occulted signifier remaining present through its (metonymic) connection with the rest of the chain.
>
> Jacques Lacan, *Écrits*

When Lacan writes about the "flash" of the metaphor, as he does here in *Écrits*, his language is already metaphoric. In constructing a trope that compares the movement of the metaphor across two images to a creative spark or a synaptic flash, in writing of the flash of the metaphor or the progression of the metonymic chain, Lacan performs a meta-linguistic act in which he effectively meta-metaphorizes the image.

What Lacan is suggesting in his description of how metaphor functions is that the flash of the metaphor occludes and overshadows that which it represents. The movement of the metaphor—a flash, a spark, a spasm— displaces the represented word and indeed would succeed in forcing it from the scene of writing altogether if it wasn't for the word's metonymic significance. That is, the image remains held in place, though temporarily eclipsed, by the force of the name.

Do you still remember the little mermaid? The image of her stumbling progress, the agonizing steps she has to take to reach her prince are, by now, occluded by the image of the knife that displaces, for a moment, our pity and terror, our image of her suffering. Displaces but not replaces, for at the same time the vision of the knife guarantees our retrieval of that first image: the little mermaid stranded on her rock, pinned there, Lacan might say, by the force of our imagination and by the flash of the metaphor traveling both backwards and forwards to construct a metonymic sequence or chain.

In "White Mythology" — to give another example of metaphoric thinking— Jacques Derrida ends his essay with a consideration of the metaphor as a heliotrope. In constructing this germinal image, Derrida positions the heliotrope as a flower growing within language, turning inevitably toward the sun that blazes with truth and light. The metaphor in western philosophy, says Derrida—and he is referring particularly to the work of Paul Ricoeur— is perceived as the potential bridge to a transcendental truth figured, in the course of his extended metaphor, as the sun toward which the flower heliotropically turns. The metaphor is both supplemental and revitalizing, it offers the possibility of language reaching past its earthly bounds toward a higher truth. Language, metaphor, writes Derrida, is always heliotropic in the sense that it is always turning to the sun, the transcendental.

I am interested, not only in how theorists seem compelled to write poetically when they turn their attention to the problem of metaphor and metonymy, but also how poets have troubled and playfully expanded our understanding of these figurative devices. One of the questions that intrigues me is whether it is possible, in fact, to write or speak other than metaphorically or metonymically since language is built upon the myriad empty crusts of hollow images that, like dying crustaceans, have shed their shells and moved on. To coin a metaphor.

RB: It is odd to be beginning this dialogue while both of us reside in BC, although you are heading back to Winnipeg. It offers an opportunity to ponder how place moves in human intentions, habits, the slick dodges of memory. How has Winnipeg stayed with you while you were gone, contrived to speak to you?

MC: I know what you mean about how place jogs memory (or maybe it's the other way around). I remember, for instance, reading a couple of books by two Winnipeg poets. I was living in Vancouver at the time—living what my friend, Cooley, persists in calling the sunless life of a scurvy west-coaster— and I had just finished re-reading Catherine Hunter's *Latent Heat* when I opened your new book, *traffick*. To the faint but persistent susurration of Vancouver winter rain I fell through the pages of these two wonderful books into a city-state-of-mind called Winnipeg.

In these poems, Hunter's narrators, like your personae, wander the "haunted, rumbling streets" of Winnipeg, a city at once familiar, local, catalogue-able:

> its twelve mighty bridges
> its pigeons, its people
> who skate on the rivers at night, gliding
> over thin ice, eyelashes
> dusted with frost
>
> Catherine Hunter, "Rush Hour"

A mysterious incalculable urban landscape as represented in "Seven Arteries," where the poet watches snow fall through "the seven levels of the city" to settle eventually upon "the dead/with gold rings on their skinny fingers,/their hair still growing underground."

Your poems, although very different in style and subject matter, are grounded, like Hunter's, in an idiosyncratic and original poetic sensibility within a city that, in less contemporary writing, has provoked all manner of wearisome, windy clichés. My favourite poem in *traffick* is "pizza guy," a long poem narrated by a canny, playful, tender and punctual deliverer of words and pizza:

> I am the pizza guy. "Poems and pepperoni," I'd say,
> apologizing for all the writing on the pizza box. "Poems and
> pizza," I'd say, hoping to sell one with the other, trick you into
> my words. Some laugh with pity, tipping a little more, hoping
> I'll get better soon, some growl and stuff the crust into their
> yawning mouths, some stare, startled by that one perfect
> word, and the pizza grows cold as it rings in their ears. Some
> speak back, sharing words over a slice or two, my other
> deliveries forgotten, sauce dribbling onto our chins.
>
> Rob Budde, "the pizza guy"

Like the melancholy angels in Wim Wenders' film, *Wings of Desire*, pizza guy eavesdrops on the lovers and insomniacs, late-night dreamers, shift-workers, nursing mothers and thieves who phone in their orders and whose lives intersect with his own; whose hunger for words, love, poetry, and pizza he satisfies in thirty minutes or less.

So, Rob, this is how "Winnipeg" has contrived to speak to me: through memory, sentiment, nostalgia, compulsion. Through speculation and scandal, news reports, no doubt exaggerated, about mosquitoes the size and ferocity of small dragons and airplanes tumbling out of the skies and onto Portage Avenue. But mostly through writing and hearsay, poems, tall stories, rumour, fulmination, and weather reports. A confusion of corners, oddly angled angels, fallen golden boys.

And *that* is the very last prepositional metaphor you will hear from me. Promise.

Todd Bruce:

The Word Inert, Expectant

The quality of mercy is not strain'd,
It droppeth as the gentle rain from heaven
Upon the place beneath; it is twice bless'd;
It blesseth him that gives and him who takes…

Shakespeare, *The Merchant of Venice* 4.1

RB: *Jiggers, Birdman, Rhapsody in D.* Although I got the order wrong by publication date, I got it right in terms of when they were written. Maybe because of that confusion, I want you to talk a little about the chronology of what you've called a trilogy.

TB: The confusion might stem from the fact that, though *Birdman* was published before *Jiggers*, it actually was written after and follows from *Jiggers*. Birdman is basically the Phoenix. The main character Jiggers dies and one of the last poems is about the parrot being burned.

My parrot flew straight into the electric heater. Got tangled in the coils. Fried to death. It was untimely. I was sad. He was purple. Had orange spots on his cheeks. This was before the heater. Quite surreal, everything about him, even his death.

The smell, my god it stunk, the smell of burnt feathers. The squawk! It was terrible. Almost plucked a tail feather but thought it might hurt. Was dead for three days before I could bring myself to touch him. I was hoping for a resurrection, parrot rising out of the ashes. I chose though, after some consideration, not to mythologize him.

Jiggers

Birdman rises out of that and it is Jiggers speaking from heaven. The entire narrative structure of *Birdman* is Jiggers speaking from heaven, which gave me great poetic license.

RB: You threw away the line in *Birdman*.

TB: I didn't throw it away, I moved away from it. There are no line breaks. *Birdman* is a narrative structure that only had the confines of the 8 1/2 x 11 page, which was very freeing.

RB: As befits heaven.

TB: Absolutely.

> The spoken word has no mass, the written is temporal. Your lifetime is the passing of a cloud once around the globe, in it, your words, angular and silent, falling into the ocean, onto this starving earth, and, at times, into the creamy shaking netted palm of a poet. Sell all that you have.
>
> *Birdman*

TB: I think what I did when I wrote *Jiggers* was that I tried to write other people's books of poetry. I assumed that if you wrote a book of poetry it had to be line structured, left-hand margin flush—it breaks away from that a bit but it wasn't experimental—it was breaking away from tradition but not in a radical way. I felt I still had to support the left-hand margin. It was my way of experimenting with the form but I didn't want to go too far away because, to be honest, I wanted to be published. I didn't want to do something too radical. To move away from that, in a justified way, into a subconscious voice or a meta-voice or ethereal voice. I just wanted to write, not to worry about structure or line breaks or rhythm or concreteness. Because I didn't feel the reader was really getting something from the structure of the poem. I wanted them to, as other poets do, I wanted them to read the silence of the white page but I think it's naïve to say that someone actually stops and experiences the blankness of the page. But I assume to contradict myself here—readers will do that. There's importance to it. There is not a single line break in that book that was not programmed into the text.

RB: Up until now you have been talking about line breaks as an imposition but you also use line breaks for effect, they amplify the text, they augment the text, they mean something.

TB: They do. I expect a student of poetry to analyze that. I do not expect a casual reader of poetry to understand that. When I read my poetry out loud I read it as though there is not that space.

RB: There's that point where the knowledge that comes out of analysis meets what you feel as you read. A line break is about time, about breath, about syntax, about reading across lines, which you can analyze and name or you can just experience.

TB: A lot of my line break decisions are based on Cooley's essay "Breaking and Entering." What he posits is that the line exists for itself first of all but the ambiguity comes in the way it connects to the next line. I was totally enthralled by that and I still am. When I read lined poetry I think of Cooley.

RB: Let's talk about some specific line breaks. This is from early on in *Jiggers*. The poem begins "neither surprised nor horrified/when you told me…"

> neither surprised nor horrified
> I wasn't I
> told you not to worry about it I'd
> take care of everything
> go ahead with your vacation I
>
> told you not to worry about it I'd
> bury him tomorrow somewhere
> you couldn't find him I
>
> listened to the drone
> of silence that tripped in after
> the connection broke

Jiggers

TB: Well, I am surprised you picked up on this. This was very difficult to write aesthetically. I wanted the "I" to be inserted yet outside it at the same time. At the time I was very conscious of the fact I wanted the "I" to be on the outside. A conscious displacement between the you and I. I hadn't done a lot of reading on the subject of "the subject" but I think I was working on that in my own way. The last thing you see is the "I" and then it collapses into the "you." I wanted the reader to see the I displaced, the poet kicked out. I don't know why.

RB: The writing subject here is unsettled, in shock, shattered, disturbed. Uncertain.

TB: It was partly a jab at the "you"—it was passive aggressive that way.

RB: Are you comfortable talking about autobiography? How much of these poems come out of experiences that you would want a reader to know? How far do you go with that?

TB: I only have my opinion. My take on the subject is that poetry is for the poet and that I would challenge any poet to tell me that their poetry is not autobiographical. I would challenge them. There is no question in my mind and I know for a fact my texts are nothing but autobiographical but I also want to give the reader an experience of poetry—I want them to engage in the language, the metaphor, the rhythm, the sound. But I don't write poetry for the reader—I write poetry for me. I honestly, for the record, do not give a flying fuck if the reader enjoys it. I am surprised I am published. It's about me and my life. Do you write for the reader?

RB: Not sure. But what do you say to the poetry student who is digging into your life to get at something behind the poem?

TB: I'd tell them the answer is in the poem. They don't know me but there is a code. It's like reading a mystery novel; if you look at this text closely there is something for you. And I am obfuscatory—I make it difficult. As a writer I encode, it's deeply encoded.

RB: You say you write for yourself but to what end?

TB: To no end actually. For me, I get a rush out of writing good poetry before the reader. It's the same rush I get when I listen to something musical that I connect to aesthetically. When I listen to a great piece of baroque music, which I am a lover of, like Bach, and get a rush, I have that emotional, internal, physical—it's the same experience I have when I am writing. It's something that feels good. So I really don't care about the reader.

RB: Is that rush intellectual or visceral?

TB: It's both. I think poets are wired that way so those are the same thing. I don't know why else I would write.

RB: Do you relate that rush to the idea of ecstasy or *jouissance*?

> Art—this semiotization of the symbolic—thus represents the flow of *jouissance* into language… In cracking the socio-symbolic order, splitting it open, changing vocabulary, syntax, the word itself, and releasing from beneath them the drives borne by vocalic or kinetic differences, *jouissance* works its way into the social and symbolic.
>
> Julia Kristeva, Revolution in Poetic Language

TB: Yeah, wouldn't you? Even when, after the fact, I look at something I've written and don't like it, when I write it, it feels good, it's a great feeling. Fuck I'm there; I'm in the zone. A little paradise. Often, and I'm going out on a limb here, if you're a decent writer and you get that rush, it's pretty good stuff.

RB: Even when it's difficult, like that passage with the isolated outside "I" that you said was difficult to write, or about love lost, is that the same sort of rush? Are there some "orgasmic" texts and some more problematic texts? You were a little dissatisfied with *Jiggers*; does that mean writing it wasn't a rush?

TB: I wrote *Jiggers* like a sound check. Does this writing wash?

     el a men tul par tik uls

     …

                        sediments metallically under

          your tongue

                        in 1 2 fil 3 4 tra 5 6 ting 7 8

                        counting is subconscious don't you

     know

                                  Jiggers

RB: You wrote *Jiggers* fairly quickly.

TB: Yeah, you were there. Delta Marsh. Let me tell you, the value of that retreat we went on was not measurable. *Jiggers* would not be written without that experience, without Cooley coming out and Kroetsch and Crozier. It was a sound check. It was a fair book of poetry but it was not Todd Bruce.

RB: It's a bit restrained.

TB: Good word—it's very restrained. And I was following the assumptions of what I had been taught.

RB: Were you writing Cooley's, Kroetsch's, and Crozier's book here?

TB: No, I was writing the Geddes anthology from first-year English. That kind of poetry.

RB: Cohen? Purdy?

TB: Purdy for sure. Of the line poets going, Purdy is one of the best.

RB: Gimme a couple more names. Birney?

TB: Yeah. Patrick Lane.

RB: Lowry, even though he wasn't writing poetry. You deny it but I see a lot of Cohen going on... Yeah. Yeah. Come on. That tragic romantic, Alice under the bridge, come on... [laughter]

TB: ...in my work? No. No. Well, okay maybe. [laughter] I guess I deny Cohen because he is such a commercial product. Okay, let the record speak, I wrote two papers on his poetry. You got me.

RB: I want to read something from Kristeva: "The text is a practice that could be compared to a political revolution. The one brings about in the subject what the other introduces into society." So when you are writing for yourself, are you in the midst of a revolution?

TB: Yes. Absolutely.

RB: Well, you have to say more than that! What, you're gonna say no?! [laughter]

TB: You know what, fuck you—this interview is over! [laughter] Yes, but not as consciously as Kristeva. She freaks me out because she gets it. I am a writer who doesn't know that. I do it. Probably can be slipped into that but when I'm writing that's not my objective. I agree with everything she says. So maybe, I don't know, Rob. I am a bit uncomfortable making myself that important, using that kind of language to describe myself. But, let's go with it. At least two of my books have challenged and I would say are small "r" revolutionary. Yes.

RB: A revolution within is just that. In your poetry, you talk about the status quo; it becomes an actor in your drama.

TB: But not capital "p" Political. It's about art. It is very political. I think art is revolution.

She was there when I lay, turning to vibrating rosewood inside his black pine piano. He played inside me. My lungs the percussion my mind the strings my heart the brass my soul the wood my eyelashes the sharp, Rachmaninoff's The Isle of the Dead. Sleep is not sleep. The touch. The trickle of ivory-spun synaptic cracks against the wood of my spine. A hollow chamber petrifying. O, the smack, my love.

Birdman

RB: Can you get more specific? What aspects are revolutionized in your texts? How would you name them in your poetry?

TB: This is the kind of conversation I love. You want to know. I think—or I believe actually—that when someone is honest in their writing and just goes with it, that's revolutionary. The revolution happens within. This is that feeling I get when I am writing. The most political texts are the ones that are honest. That's hard to define. We're talking about Elizabeth Smart, Clarice Lispector… It doesn't have to be negative to be revolutionary but it usually is.

I am standing on a corner in Monterey, waiting for the bus to come in, and all the muscles of my will are holding my terror to face the moment I most desire.

Elizabeth Smart, *By Grand Central Station*
I Sat Down and Wept

RB: Negative in what way?

TB: In the fact that it's sad. It hurts. It hurts to write, to live it.

RB: It hurts to resist something?

TB: It hurts to be honest about your life. That's a basic representation of what pop psychology is, but it's true. It's confession. Foucault was all over it. Telling the truth of oneself. That's brutally difficult to do. I think poets do that.

RB: What I want to put pressure on in your instance is, when you are honest, what types of things are unveiled? Just to nudge it, what does honesty have to do with language? How does language speak honestly?

TB: When I am being honest with content, I find the poetics rise to cover or veil. When I am telling the truth of myself, and Foucault calls it the "technology of the self," I find that my poetics—and I hate to institute a hierarchy—but my poetics elevate. I have access to a different kind of language.

RB: Especially in *Jiggers* and *Rhapsody*, the honesty seems to lie in the expression of loss. Your confession is that emotion.

TB: It was very challenging in *Jiggers* because while there is loss going through the whole book, the loss at the end is the loss of self because the narrator dies. That's why I wrote *Birdman*, to say, okay, here I am, I am lost.

> 11/11/90
> noon?
>
> cold wind like snow
> stove eating wood like
> a stove eating wood
>
> a dead pelican this morning
> frozen in the lake
> its webbed feet frozen
> it tried to leave
> something got at it
> just below the neck
> wolf I guess
> scared away though
> wonder why

Jiggers

RB: Who is the "I" who writes the diary entries, Jiggers or the narrator? It's unclear.

TB: You want an answer to that?

RB: Not necessarily.

TB: If I was forced to answer the question—it is Jiggers, but back in time when he is at the cottage and he's healthy. It's normal and he's just writing in his diary. It's banal. It's him writing not as a poet, not as somebody who's dying, it's him being normal, a dad, someone at the cottage. I wanted to give him that voice because he has all the other tragic voices. I wanted to give him some normalcy. At the cottage, the fire is burning, I am out of wood, the fox is dead…

RB: That's very Kroetschian to include that diary.

TB: I know he is an extremely strong presence in my writing.

RB: Tell me if I am wrong, but Elizabeth Smart and Robert Kroetsch, from the outside, seem to be the most prevalent influences on your writing.

TB: Absolutely. Smart for her style and Kroetsch for his content. Not to take away from Kroetsch's style, but it is unreadable sometimes.

RB: The formal attributes of his poetry seem to be something you emulate. This diary entry...

TB: I was mimicking.

RB: Smart has a type of lush, almost grandiose, elevated...

TB: ...textured, rich...

RB: ...rich, but screeching, screaming, howling writing that you capture quite often. It rages.

TB: I am enraged! [laughter] I think honestly we've undervalued, underestimated Smart's writing as Canadians.

RB: Besides *By Grand Central Station I Sat Down and Wept,* should we be reading anything else?

TB: *Rogues and Rascals.* Well, no, I'll be honest, nothing comes close to *By Grand...*but *By Grand...*is one of the best examples you can point to in terms of poetic prose. It's called a novel but I think it's a poem.

RB: Are there other examples of that kind of poetic prose like *Birdman*?

TB: Not in Canada, but Clarice Lispector's *The Stream of Life.* There's *The Bell Jar* by Sylvia Plath. All of sudden there's going to be a connection that these are all very depressing. But maybe the best poetic prose is depressing.

RB: Why is that?

TB: I think prose is the best genre for lamenting. I've read some good lamenting line poems but they don't have the same structure, saturation, melancholy. That's why I moved into poetic prose. *Rhapsody* is poetic prose too. I break into lines occasionally. I don't think you can get the same feel for what the narrator wants you to feel if you break the line.

RB: I want to talk around this for a while—the idea of lament, elegy, requiem. These revolve around your content. Why is that? Why are you attracted to that kind of story?

TB: First of all, there is the truth of it. I've lived through some tragedy. So you write what you know. I am looking for sympathy but I lived through some real shit in my life. For me as a poet, it was a natural expression of what I was feeling. But that's not the case now. *Jiggers* was not that depressing.

RB: Well, committing suicide by cutting one's ankles?

TB: I stole that from Ondaatje in *Coming through Slaughter.*

RB: Oh, the whores. And where did Mary come in?

TB: She was my uncle Jiggers' girlfriend named Mary.

RB: Was she Cree or Ojibwe or Métis?

TB: Métis. And I had a friend, Jane Peloquin, who knew a lot about the traditions and she helped me through that. I think you wrote a review in which you question my use of the "Earth Mother"—you didn't like that I used an aboriginal woman as an earth mother.

RB: I think I said I didn't think it was wrong but I was nervous about it because it was idealizing and any idealizations can be dangerous.

TB: I didn't idealize her. As a poet you fight all kinds of criticism: no it's not true, I am making it up or, it is true so fuck you, I did it right. But, was I misrepresenting the voice of a Métis woman? I don't know. That was my experience. I embellished. She didn't teach me about the chamomile plant. You know my attraction to floral imagery. I am driven to that. She was a way of getting there.

RB: But she's quite a central figure, magical…

TB: She's a witch. [sound of beer spilling] Everything's okay, nobody panic!! [pause]

RB: Well, maybe a medicine woman. There's a problem in translation there. Maybe that's why I was nervous in the review. The danger of misrepresentations.

TB: I am writing a novel now and I have a character who is white but she practises traditional aboriginal medicine, philosophy, religion, whatever you want to call it. And I thought, can I get away with this? Now it's easier. Everyone is practising.

RB: My experience in talking with aboriginal scholars and teachers and students and the way the cultures have been so besieged by misrepresentations has been that it's hard for them to have any sense of their own culture because of all the clutter, deliberate or not.

TB: I defer to you on the subject and...

RB: I am just explaining the review and the question and why I raise it.

TB: At the time of *Jiggers* I did a lot of research into Cree syllabics and tried to get them into the text but they couldn't, at that time, typeset them.

RB: I have no high moral ground. Most of *Misshapen* is from the point of view of an African American woman. It just needs to be addressed.

I am going to veer off. I come back to a phrase near the end of *Jiggers*. You say there that you "have a problem with language." Could you talk about that problem with language? As a poet who uses language, how can you have a problem with language?

I was described as "shocking" the other day. Of course, this came as a complete surprise to me when in fact my life is a response to how shocked I am, at every moment, by the status quo.

> *Still Life:*
> how impossible it seems,
> these words, next to
> one another. But then
> again, I have a problem
> with language.
>
> Still,
> I use it.
> You can tell,
> of course,
> I am weary, tired after all.
> Tough place to be, here is.
>
> *Jiggers*

TB: Those six words, "I have a problem with language," are pretty much the crux of my poetics. High five to you! [slap] Those again are not my words. In *The Lovely Treachery of Words*, Kroetsch says nearly the same thing. I hate to be slobbering over Kroetsch all the time but this is genius. When I read those words, I stopped. For me that's the truth. The reason I write is that I have a problem with language. I want to work that problem out. And I don't think in terms of Aristotle where this happened and then this happened. I think more like Plato where there is this vast encompassing problem and I don't know the answer but I have to deal with the question. As a poet, I have a problem with language so that's why I am a poet. I keep banging away at it. I think language is more than structure. I think it's more than story-telling. I think it's also about rhythm and music and form and clay and...

RB: Magic?

TB: I am afraid of admitting to it in public. Yes, that's what it comes down to. What matters to me is what I figure out in terms of structure and rhythm. It's about me figuring out my problem with language. It's a chess game; it's a puzzle. I studied poetry so much, I feel safe moving outside that. I feel more secure working with language. But I first had to fuck with it. Like Rabelais. I had to fight this structure.

RB: Or confronting the structure so that it becomes a structure. Instead of taking it as natural.

TB: Mark Wigley. I had to confront the structure of language. That's what contemporary poetry is all about. All poetry. Just look at Milton or Chaucer.

RB: Chaucer maybe, not so sure about Milton. To me, he seems pretty secure with the structure...

TB: Well, Chaucer then. I think I have that problem. I want to push language to its edges and then let it come back to me. Now I can work with it.

RB: I am finding that novel writing has the same type of problem with language but is dealing not just with language but also metalanguage. I have a problem with language, I have a problem with story.

TB: Yes, a different register. I am not a natural novel writer. This is a painful experience. I could write you a poem [bang] tonight. But this novel writing thing is a bitch. But I am compelled to do it. I no longer have the same problem with language I used to have—I have pressed, I've compressed, I've done some weird shit, I have worked it out over three books. Now, I have a problem with story.

RB: What can poetry do that philosophy or psychoanalysis cannot? I know you read a lot of Derrida, Kristeva, Foucault.

TB: Tough one. You could argue they are not so different. Depends who you are reading. They also write about poetry. What they taught me is how to read poetry. Foucault especially.

RB: What texts?

TB: *Technologies of the Self.* I am trying to avoid being dramatic about the whole thing. You ask a really difficult question.

RB: Go back to the Kristeva quote. Would theory then describe "the revolution"?

TB: Or hope to. They would draw a shadow of it. Kristeva talks about "phenotext" and "genotext." Poetry would be genotext. Theory still is phenotext. There is no way of getting into that raw, DNA space of it. We can interpret it. The schism. That's all we can hope for.

> The phenotext is a structure…it obeys rules of communication
> and presupposes a subject of enunciation and addressee. The
> genotext, on the other hand, is a process; it moves through zones
> that have relative and transitory borders and constitutes a *path*
> that is not restricted to the two poles of univocal information
> between two full-fledged subjects.

> Julia Kristeva, *Revolution in Poetic Language*

I have been thinking these last couple of days about what you'd ask me here and I had no idea. I knew you'd fuck me up. [laughter]

RB: I didn't plan this. This is the truth. I was making notes on your book and in the car I accidentally turned a page and found that Kristeva quote from *Revolution*. On the way here. Honest. Honest. [laughter]

TB: I can't speak for other poets. I know for certain that Dennis Cooley and I are very different poets. I don't get the sense that it's as intense for him. For me poetry is an extremely intense, emotional, psychological experience. I've tried writing it. In the novel I am writing called "Home Street," one of the characters is an artist, a potter, and I get to use her experience of creating art as how I experience creating poetry, so I got to write it down. I can't explain it, Rob. It's almost like you go nuts. It works in terms of sound and rhythm and sexuality and structure and feeling. Please don't ask me to explain it.

RB: What do you say to a student who says, the poem just is, I don't want to analyze it?

TB: I don't buy that. I think that's a cop-out. There's more to it. I think it's bad reading. I am not overly articulate about my own poetry...

RB: There's a lot going on. The author doesn't always know all that's going on.

TB: I hope not. Sometimes I write just for freedom.

RB: I am going to read another Kristeva passage: "Magic, shamanism, esoterism, the carnival, the incomprehensible, poetry all underscore the limits of socially useful discourse and attest to what it represses; the process that exceeds the subject and its communicative structures."

TB: The process. When I am in process that exceeds truth. Process is aesthetics. That's where we come to joy. You almost have to talk about it spiritually and you know I resist that...

RB: That's the next question (teasing).

TB: I resist it, but—if I was going to be perfectly honest and you are the only person I am completely honest with—I think it's spiritual. It's my communion with whoever I am. Once in a while I connect with myself, not with a God.

RB: We've bumped heads over spirituality before. I am interested in the word "transubstantiation" and the idea that this here, what I am taking, IS the body and blood of Christ. And I am thinking of the last line of *Jiggers:* "To touch my body." We are talking about spirituality and magic. That excess that Kristeva is talking about, could that be a type of transubstantiation?

> an unfolding of ink
> is all
>
> a listening
> an echo
>
> a remembering
> to forget
>
> an invitation
> to tea and biscuits
>
> to a tolling of bells

> to taste my breath
>
> to touch my body

Jiggers

TB: I want to be like Peter and say yes. My initial response is yes. But I've become more guarded, so…

RB: Especially in *Rhapsody*, it seems to me you are trying to access a body, you are trying to allow the reader to taste that body. Which would be miraculous.

> the mellifluous tongue of god and, perhaps, you have kissed
> the feet of Christ

> And. The power of your absence is obscene.

> All that is left is the blatant sun.

> [the power of silence
>
> the extracted blood…]

Rhapsody in D

> On the clothesline in your backyard sits the Red Sacred
> Swallow. Legend has it that her red throat is a reminder
> that she has pulled a thorn from Christ's crown as he
> hung (defunct) on the cross. She remembers how he
> saw his reflection in the brimming grail, how he
> whispered to himself, "this is my blood." She
> remembers his astounded eyes.

Rhapsody in D

TB: I never dreamed anyone would pick up on those complications. Tincture means if you are kneeling you take communion on the tongue. The narrator believes that taking communion by tincture is more pure. What are you really asking me?

RB: That's it, I don't know.

TB: I am a man who hides my faith. In the same way I am a poet; it is my experience. My experience of the divine, my understanding of the divine is very private. But I throw it out into my writing all the time. *Rhapsody* was especially difficult because Dan, who I am writing the book about, was very devout. When I write about God, or the possibility of God, or the realm of religion, I don't know if that is some kind of subconscious, primordial instinct but...when I want to create I find myself going toward that kind of poem because anything can happen, Rob.

RB: Might you be pointing in that direction because that is where language fails? Like death. Language comes to this edge...

TB: ...cul de sac...then there are no rules.

> (and) we fail, like the poem, to be silent
> to be and
> to enter the texture (of love)
>   my love, my only one, is to die

Rhapsody in D

RB: Your problem with language is finding those spaces where language fails, that failing structure.

TB: That's interesting. I think it's true.

RB: Reading some more, this time from *Jiggers*: "when you do/not come to me/I feel you/the most when I/build the blank sky a fortress."

TB: Actually it reads "when you do not come to me I feel you the most."

RB: Yeah, whatever! Get rid of the line breaks then.

It's about absence, memory, and recovery. It seems to me that this might be a unified to notion in your text. Absence makes one feel more intensely. All sorts of profound absences in the text. Absence and the other. And I think it is connected to romance. You say yourself in *Rhapsody*, "I am a romantic."

TB: You're hitting all the hot spots. The other-than is a place you can never access. I am drawing on all sorts, mixing my metaphors, muddling my sources. There's Heidegger, there's Derrida, there's Levinas. I guess what I am trying to articulate in that kind of poetics is a deep loss. Loss that you know you can never retrieve. An absence so huge you can't ever possibly cross the chasm to it. But it's like unrequited love. The other-than is the part of the self that you can't retrieve. A huge gap. I think my poetics revolves around what that means. The idea of the outside of the "I." Rob it's a huge force but you can't identify it. You can't say, "You are it." You are the other-than. Part of my use of those philosophical texts was to say I am confused by it. But instinctually and emotionally, it means something to me because it was taught to me by somebody I trust—Dawne McCance. And she said to me, "Just work with it." The capital "O" Other is the other in the social contract via Rousseau. The small "o" other is the other of the self that you can't identify. Don't quote me—that's for the scholars. It's very complicated. Occasionally you "get it." It's almost spiritual. You celebrate it. It's mystical. It's certainly not pejorative.

> [for you I will dislodge
> the sun from the sky]
>
> *Rhapsody in D*

RB: I want to get back to these lines though. One of the things they suggest is that, in the absence of the other, I am going to build monuments.

TB: The monument I had in mind was the Taj Mahal. I wanted to erect monuments in my mind, in my aesthetic experience. I want to catalogue those moments and that was one of them. I want to be able to say I had a great mind fuck and erect a monument to that. One of the things we do as poets is mummify. We preserve.

RB: I guess I was thinking along different lines. I was thinking of displacement. The loss of the other, the inability to have that presence, leads to a displacement, a creative act. I am getting Lacan screwed in here, I think. Some of the poems are about, yes, memorial, but also an anti-memorial. A counter-movement. An inaccessibility. In that absence, we create.

TB: I trust you. I see the seed, but say more. In death there is profound presence?

RB: You pull out in the poems an access to the subject-in-process. Because of your honesty and freedom. The idea of subjecthood is a type of original loss, or fundamental loss because we are unable to access the other. We are in mourning.

TB: The poet as lost poet.

> One of these days I'll fall. Free fall. Perhaps I will survive.
>
> *Rhapsody in D*

Dennis Cooley:
Dreaming His Way into the World

This interview was originally published in *Prairie Fire*, a special issue on Dennis Cooley (Vol.19, No. 1 Spring, 1998)

RB: We're sitting at Carlos and Murphy's in Winnipeg. There it is. Todd Bruce, Dennis Cooley, and Rob Budde. Start.

TB: Tell me how a Cooley poem starts.

DC: They can start in lots of ways. They almost always start off with some other text, which wouldn't necessarily be a printed text, but off some language, somewhere. I remember one time for example watching a program on television about those little insects in the carpets, dust mites. They would throw themselves on some kind of a prong and I wrote a poem off that. But one way or another they almost always involve texts, though some of them will come off some fairly strong personal experiences. I've written how many poems now about death; I wrote a poem about my dad and a poem about my mom, though even as you write those, you start sneaking around looking at other texts. Mostly it's something that I read. I'm often locally influenced. I'll read Sharon Olds and say, I really like this! And write what seems to me a poem influenced by Sharon Olds, but may not be obvious to anybody else.

RB: So is it usually a response? When you read that Sharon Olds, are you picking up on something that she is doing and responding to it, or rearticulating it?

DC: A kind of syntax or a way of constructing a sentence. Often it's things you don't do yourself, at least for me, that excite me, saying, "How did she do that?!" or "I don't know how to do that!" I'm often more impressed by people who write things that are quite different and I end up with a sense of discovery and amazement.

TB: The way you respond to *As for Me and My House* seems to me is different from the way you respond to someone like Sharon Olds. With Ross's novel you have a really strong background text and you respond to it in terms of its philosophy, I think, rather than in terms of its innovation.

DC: Yeah, it's more general terrain with the Ross pieces in that I'm not even terribly interested in that text as I write the poems, it's more kind of psychological—it's a situation I play off and with, usually a series that tends to be more comical, more parodic, also more erotic, more emotional. Though they are still tailored to a great extent by that positioning of that female figure as she knocks things around in her head. I find texts to play off and with, like the space texts of the astronauts and cosmonauts, and Dracula texts; fighting them in various ways. Writing this ridiculous pile of Dracula poems.

TB: Which texts, structurally, influence you the most?

DC: I guess the long poem, especially the Canadian long poem. It has its origins in all kinds of places, among them certainly, obviously, in Pound and Eliot, William Carlos Williams, who has been an enormous influence on me.

RB: e.e. cummings too, I think.

DC: Yeah, yeah, yeah, and Barrie Nichol, of course, in some ways—probably he or his friends would be really offended at the suggestion—but I think there's some connections there between cummings and Nichol even. Nichol tends to run out of a continental surrealism, Dadaism, and so on, more so, but I think there are some important connections.

RB: In terms of poetics it seems to me that there's something that you share. When you were talking about hearing something strange, and something done differently, I was thinking about how I often see your poems leaping out of a few words, how you'll kind of unfold a phrase, or a way of speaking, and then you'll go through it and over it and then fold in the rhymes and sounds and puns, all springing out of that one thing. It seems to me bp Nichol has that awareness of language.

DC: Yeah. Though he commits himself more fully to doing what we used to call "sound poetry" than I do. I do some of it, but he did a lot more of it than I do. I also like the referent, you know. I had this very quarrel with him one time. We were having a beer years ago when he was in Winnipeg, and he was arguing about the reflexivity of language, I was saying, yeah, of course there's that, but words do mean, they do have references! And that is not insignificant in texts! I know you can't have it at the same time, but I want reference and I want syntactical surprise and breakage and crazy puns and syllables freed loose and I want emotion and I want parody. I want it all. In all the things I've written, there's a kind of mix of those things. Sometimes I wonder if that hasn't something to do with the response, or lack of response, to the writing I've done. It's pretty hard to say what would be a "typical" poem.

TB: When you do spread it out on the page, when you give all this space to the text, and let the words sort of scatter across the page, stars or commas or whatever: is that a political statement?

DC: Well, stating the obvious, all writing is political; you'll never be outside the political; or perhaps a better term might be "ideological position." But I don't think of it simply as an inevitability. There clearly are political implications for how you structure a text. One of the consequences of scattering words on the page, or not offering a certain kind of pact through a text, is that it will give your readers a lot of permission but it also puts a lot of pressure on them. Many readers don't like that, which puzzles me. I mean, what a wonderful position to be in as a reader! But I think some people get really angry about that.

TB: Are you refusing convention?

DC: No, you can never be outside of convention. What you can do is do different things, you push them, but it's actually impossible to be outside of convention. Even if theoretically you could be at the end of a range of intelligibility, if you ever could get there, you'd be unintelligible to anybody, right? There are conventions for making meaning, and however you may push them, wherever you may take them, you're always playing inside conventions. You might push them, alter them, try out new possibilities, but that's all.

TB: I respect the fact that you're a poet who remains a poet. Was it a conscious decision not to branch out into the mainstream, into prose? So many novelists began as poets; never, or seldom, do they return. What do you think that this is due to?

DC: A lot of people, especially young writers, begin in poetry, and I guess there are some obvious and very practical reasons, particularly if you're involved in a writing community or a course or workshop or with friends or whatever, so you're going to generate texts in short order, what can you generate? You can generate poems, they're short! And they involve some entry into language, where you're trying out possibilities, so that in many ways poetry is a good site of apprenticeship, whatever it is you may do.

But I don't think the boundary has to be that sharp. You look at the people who as poets went into writing prose fiction. They'll often write a different kind of prose fiction, I think, than some others. One could argue that Ondaatje's novels are—whatever this may mean—more poetic than novels written by people who have never written poetry.

TB: So why do you stay in the genre? Why don't you go outside it?

DC: I don't know if I would have the patience to build a great big structure, that you need to do when you write a novel.

RB: *Bloody Jack* is as big a structure as...

DC: Yeah, but you can enter in a different way. The form I love is the long poem. I also love lyrics and all kinds of things, but the long poem allows you to do so many things. That may be where I do something that has some connection with a novel, but there you have to have a big, overarching structure to do something with those multi-voiced forms that *Bloody Jack* uses.

I remember when I was doing it, Arnason and Kroetsch were—Kroetsch especially—after me to make it more narrative. I'd show them things along the way, and Kroetsch would say, "Tell the story! What's the story of this guy?" When Arnason assembled the pieces shortly before publication, he grabbed most of the narrative things and stuck them in. On the sly, I took out some of those and re-inserted some love poems. And a lot of the metalingual pieces got lost, I probably had about twenty pages. Looking back, I wish a few more of them had got in.

I like being able to make those multiple and brief entries, really mobile entries. Even with a pretty radical novel, you still have to worry about some kind of large structure, what you've got and what you're building, whereas a long poem just allows you to put in anything you want, I like to believe. But I also just like that intense involvement with language, of doing something with language, and let's face it, a lot of novels have pages of pretty ordinary writing, pretty ordinary language.

TB: In terms of the structure, I don't see you as working on a focused idea for a long period of time. It seems to me it's a poem and then another poem and then another poem. But, are you always working on a big idea when you're writing?

DC: I work in series a lot, and I work on them simultaneously. So right now I'm working on some stuff that's been around for years and years, but to identify some of the more recent things, I've been working on a series of related Dracula poems, "love in a dry land"—those poems that play off the Ross text, a long poem about my mom's death—there are a couple more in there. I'm working on a couple of journals—I work on a lot of projects at the same time. But I often find a kind of area that I mine, even in individual poems. Typically I'll begin with a pretty small thing, and I'll commonly amplify, and say, what are the possibilities in this? Very common process. And then sometimes I'll say, oh shit, I've got to cut this back. But I tend to write something and say, where could I take this?

RB: "Mine" is an interesting verb to use, especially coming from Estevan.

DC: You say, what are your options? If you believe in the inspirational model solely, it seems to me you get yourself into trouble in a big hurry. Because how often is a poem going to hit you out of the blue, BANG!? How you generate writing becomes an issue. One of the things to do is a series, you find an area that excites you in some way or other, or speaks to you in exciting ways that are filled with possibilities. And you say, what have I got here? So Dracula, vampire, are there other vampires around, are there related figures, this is a Victorian construction, what about Victorian narratives, what sense of gendering have we got here, you've got a circulation system, you start in on blood. And so—we've got this guy, this "Red," who's intervening in the circulation system, in the currency of Her Majesty's realm. And Dracula starts becoming the Commie, or a Red, right? And you can go on and on and on just like that.

TB: A more complicated question might be when does the series end?

RB: Cooley does not know how to answer that question!

DC: Arnason comes in and takes it away. [laughter] I don't think you ever know when it's done. I've heard versions of this in various places, and one of the most recent that I read that I really like is an essay by Barbara Johnson. She talks about simple exhaustion, boredom, whatever, where you kind of run out of steam, or you get drawn over somewhere else. And it's just sheer accident, the world is more or less a series of accidents, I think. You might have spent the rest of your life and written nine thousand more pages or suddenly you've got another idea, and you run with something else.

TB: OK, then, how do you know what the last line of a poem is?

DC: Well, it depends on how strong a sense of closure you want, for one thing. I generally don't like very strong closures. The ones that are more emotional or intimate, I'll be willing to have a little stronger sense of closure, partly because I'm investing myself in poignancy. The "love in a dry land" series will more often have a stronger sense of closure than in, say, *Bloody Jack*, where there's another one, there's another one, there's another one. But I don't like a really strong sense of closure, as a rule. At least I'm wary of it, I guess. In *Bloody Jack* clearly there's Cooley saying, How am I going to end this thing? And he stutters a series of closures. And in the end, he says to the reader, You do it! I'm leaving, it's in your hands.

TB: Kroetsch says somewhere that poets are defined by the fact that they have a problem with language. What I've always assumed is that when poets stop having a problem with language, they move on into the more narrative structures, more linear things, more conventional things. I'm not saying that's a good thing, I think they're under the illusion that they've gone past their problem. You stay with your problem with language.

DC: The problem doesn't have to be a painful one, though. Easily one of my greatest, most constant pleasures is writing. I steal occasions to play with a few words or lines and it is a kind of ecstasy—it's also a kind of driven thing, I'm kind of obsessive in some ways about it. But I enormously love writing and revising and thinking about possibilities and making notes and reading other texts, often in a kind of crazy misreading—have you ever had that experience, where you're reading along and you expect that the next word's going to be this and it's not? That kind of false expectation, misreading, often generates text for me. Or other possibilities. But I love writing!

RB: I just want to backtrack a bit. We talked about passion for poetry, we talked about the play and the pleasure in poetry, but we began by saying that all writing is political. So now where do those two meet? If the idea that writing is a problem with language—you say that it's play with language —do you have a problem with language, is there some kind of thing you're trying to do with language to teach, to change the way language is?

DC: I doubt if I could do that, I don't think many people can. I think very few people can really alter what a poem might be, much less what language is or might be. The most drastic entries even in some ways are pretty small peanuts in the history and the structure of a language, especially with something like English. It's so volatile and so omnivorous; it has taken on so many formations. You can only make really small entries in it in many ways. So I certainly don't fancy that I'm altering the face of poetry in any particular way. I don't think of myself as someone who influences other people particularly as a poet. I guess if I think of myself consciously as someone who might influence, it would be as pedagogue, probably. I guess one of my perennial projects is to try and get people reading poetry with some interest and excitement and intelligence and respect, that these things matter and you can read poems and they're important—I've lost track of the question. [laughter]

RB: Going back to the beginning of the question, which you haven't really dealt with: how is your writing political?

DC: Oh, in multiple ways. One of the ways is trying out, both as writer and as reader of texts, certain kinds of voices that might enter and might become honoured in a literary world. So an interest in oral language and vernacular language, I think, is part of it. And often those voices will come from people who wouldn't have thought of themselves as particularly literary or literate, much less poetic. But I really like that sort of thing, and I've tried to bring that into play, into my theoretical arguments, too. You're saying these too are possibilities in life, not simply solemn singularity or steadfastness, those who seriously count up the debits and credits—these aren't the only options in the world, and yet those get named in our world as real. And play, in particular, gets named as unreal. You know that Freudian distinction—the opposite of the real is not the unreal but play. So the reality principle for him in many ways is a world of prohibition and limitation and denial, and this is not real but in certain ways destructive of a certain kind of creativity. It's scandalous.

TB: I think being a poet necessarily means you are political, of course, but it also means that you're anti-establishment.

DC: I think it would be for most forms of poetry, at least in our culture. Even pretty cautious poetry is improper in our culture.

TB: The way that you structure your poems really bamboozles the reader, you're just exploding words onto the page, scattering them. I talked to Manuela Dias at Turnstone Press just today about typesetting your poems, and she said it's a nightmare. So that's even beyond the anti-establishment of being a poet in the first place. Going that further step and exploding language onto the page in a way that is very unconventional seems to me another political statement.

DC: Yeah, though there are people who will do versions of this more drastically even. It strikes me that the difference between what I am doing and what some other people are doing, is that others would tend to choose more particularly in the field, and I'm more inclined to say I want to try on almost anything. And in fact try to bring into play several of those things at the same time. So some of those very poems will be poems that might well be, say, very emotional pieces, where there's also a dislocation of language which might put a reader into crisis, or uncertainty, but they may be poems that express, at least for me, some very powerful emotions at the same time.

TB: When you sit down to write now, is it the same as when you sat down to write years ago?

DC: No. The first things I wrote tended to be more biographical, more representational, more imagist-based.

TB: And now—

DC: Well, I'm just doing more and more things. I like Atwood's argument. I don't think that after a certain point you get better. You learn things however you learn things, and then you do things, and you can learn more information and more tricks and stuff. I remember Wayne Tefs saying to me at one point, "It looks to me like your writing is changing," and I said, "No, it's been there all along." The things that you're seeing, that are appearing, are of a certain kind, but that strain's been there from the start, too.

RB: Often people argue that someone like Michael Ondaatje has gotten better as a writer because he's gained international fame, and yet I know you would argue that something like *The Collected Works of Billy the Kid* is his best work.

DC: It's interesting, I think some of the most varied texts come from people fairly early in their career. Arnason's best text, I've argued all along, is *Marsh Burning*. Certainly the one in which he pushes himself hardest and tries out most possibilities. I mean, he's gotten slicker in some ways, and he always is very smart about things, but that text is the one that is the most impressive.

TB: Do you feel put out by the fact that people see *Bloody Jack* as your best text?

DC: I wouldn't be.

TB: Is that fair? Is *Bloody Jack* your best?

DC: Well, it might be, it's not for me to decide. I certainly remember as I wrote it, saying to myself very clearly as I did it: "This will be the most important book I'll ever write." Which is not the same thing, necessarily. It certainly is the most ambitious. The thing is, practicalities have an enormous force: no one will publish a book of poetry that long any more. So it certainly wouldn't offend me if people thought that. I would be disappointed if they didn't read anything else but that.

RB: Many readers have come into a lot of joy from your writing, and celebrate it. We've seen it in the things that have come in for this issue already. Meanwhile you claim you haven't influenced anybody. I think you'll see as you read through this issue all the imitations, all the people who are taking on a Cooleyesque voice. It's quite astounding to see. And it's been there all along, these aren't just invented for this occasion.

DC: Well you know, this issue really matters a lot to me. Writing needs forms of attention, and they can be multiple. Without them a lot of writing just will go nowhere. There won't be readership unless there are various ways of attending upon it. And this is one of the important sites that invites attention, saying, "you might want to look at something here." All of poetry needs these types of forums.

RB: So what you're basically arguing is that in order for poetry to survive, we have to build a community first, in some way?

DC: We need them all at the same time. Without venues, you're not going to have it! One of the things that happened in the mid-seventies is that we started a whole bunch of venues.

RB: You're speaking of Turnstone Press. What other things?

DC: *CV2* got underway about that time, and *Border Crossings* started as *Arts Manitoba*—institutions absolutely crucial for literature.

RB: So magazines, the Manitoba Writers' Guild—

DC: *Prairie Fire*—it's crucial to have these things.

RB: Something as simple as the closing down of Merk's I think has a profound effect. I run into young writers and I want to try and direct them to some place where they can come to talk to writers, and it's difficult. We don't have Merk's any more.

DC: That's right! Merk's was an important literary institution. With the academy being so squeezed in these parts for years, with there being no new hirings, that's made an enormous difference, because the academy will often provide a site out of which things can happen, with people who have some kind of income and who are involved full time. Again, I wince when I hear what seem to be insidious blind attacks on "the academics"—what does that mean? and what are the consequences of saying this? A really healthy literary world would have academic participation, even in practical ways:

someone's got an income and a job, a literary job. And that site can be the basis for all kinds of literary events.

RB: I had to address that quite a few years ago. We were talking about resistance to poetry, and I remember confronting a few figures in the writing community, "downtown" writers, who had been very resistant to your presence in the writing community, and I was confused by that. A lot of their issues had to do with the fact that the university is a place of privilege that they don't have access to. And as a university student sometimes I forgot that, that I needed that $3,000 a year that a lot of people didn't have. It dawned on me that maybe there is some cause for jealousy or some resentment for that privilege. It was a difficult stage I was going through, trying to figure this out.

DC: At the same time, the literary folks at the University of Manitoba have been active supporters of the Writers' Guild and *Prairie Fire* and the conferences and the readings and have published all kinds of people in the community.

TB: I want to talk about some poetry! You know what I want to know about? The poem "I.O.U." (*Bloody Jack*). I want to know how it was built, I want to know what came first, I want to know everything about that poem.

DC: Well as best I can remember, I had constructed the figure of U as a character in *Bloody Jack* as someone driven by rage and jealousy, largely of a sexual sort, and had my idea, my notion of an "I.O.U." as some principle of power or indebtedness or retribution. I wanted to do many things, including concrete poems, and so it kind of suggested itself. An "I.O.U" as a sense of some relationship, and I've got this play of letters which become pronouns so I could build a kind of power structure there in the geography of the poem, that squeezes it into a little corner. Doesn't the "U" squeeze, trickle out somehow? and finally, the "I"—isn't the "I" in large case and the "U" in lower case, that kind of power relationship, that desire to contain, and escape in that containment as well?

RB: But it's also making a statement about the materiality of language. Which a lot of your poems do. Quite often that seems to be a central issue, in some ways either the materiality of the word, the sentence, the line. I'm thinking of the poem "the end of the line."

> reached out to send you this line
> out to send you this line reached
> to send you this line reached out
> send you this line reached out to

> you this line reached out to send
> this line reached out to send you
> line reached out to send you this

Bloody Jack

And I'm thinking of your signature, your physical signature in *Bloody Jack*, things like that, the physical nature of language.

DC: Yeah. It's also kind of a constant acknowledgement that you don't have—never have—simple naked representation. That desire I think provides the basis for the frustrations I think some readers have in reading this text, of wanting to believe that you can simply testify, for example. You can never be outside of the medium. And that scandalizes and offends and angers a lot of people.

RB: And again that desire for communication and message. I'm thinking of a poem in *Bloody Jack* that ends "barely making it (up)"—making it up, lying, telling tall tales, it runs all through your poetry.

```
                    im making it
        up
           all right
              its hard
                 making
        it up
                    up &
        making
              it
                 making
                             up
              yup
           getting up
        pity
              making
                 just bare
              ly mak
                    ing
        it
                    (up)
```

Bloody Jack

TB: You're always having fun with the reader. *Bloody Jack*—it's a comedy in a lot of ways. And then, all of a sudden, ping! you hit us with a lyric, with the power of "By the Red." You know it's one of my favourite poems. Well, we get to that poem and we're just smashed into this incredible oblivion of sorrow and pain and desire and hope and tenderness. I can see the poem, it swings in my mind. When you're writing that part of the poem, is that difficult for you?

DC: I remember once I was well into the text and Daphne Marlatt—she came here as our writer-in-residence—and I showed her what I had and she said, "This can't be all about the same character, because some of them are funny and rambunctious, and some of them are tender," and I said, "Sure!" I was actually surprised that she of all people would have said that. And I said, "Well yeah!" And that's me, too, right? I enjoy the most trivial and silly jokes, and I like crazy ideas, and I'm a sucker for emotion.

RB: If anything I find you oscillate between those two things—a kind of a tenderness, mourning, tender love poems, poems about your own body, those kinds of poems, and then there's laughter, the trickster, bawdiness, tomfoolery, those two things—that's not fair, because there's many things outside that, but those two things stick out for me as trends all through your writing career.

DC: Yeah, I would have identified those lines myself.

RB: Which is a wonderful combination.

TB: I want to go out on a bit of a limb here. It seems to me that for you there is a constant leitmotif of your relationship to sunlight. Could you say a bit about that?

DC: I've been coming back to it again and again and again. I'm suspicious of geographical or biographical explanations, but there may be something here. I come from Estevan, as you know, which has the highest average hours of sunshine of any place in Canada. So I grew up in a world that was a huge sky filled with light. Always. Whether that has anything to do with it, I don't know.

TB: Do you consciously mythologize the sun?

DC: I probably do ultimately. What does it mean, what does a myth mean? In the most obvious sense of the word, I like to believe I don't mythologize much of anything. I guess I do that with Jack in certain ways, but not by making him some version of a Greek hero, or somebody that you'd read about in Jung. He's a kind of anti-hero, almost.

RB: More sensual than mythological to me. You know what just popped into my head? Lorna Crozier's poem, "On the Seventh Day."

DC: I read it in Germany, and they just loved it! [laughter] They roared!

RB: And then that last line, something like "that thin spit of land beneath that huge prairie sky."

DC: Yeah, yeah! There it is, there's a prairie poem for you. Getting back to the sun: Arnason has somewhere in his Rene Descartes poem—this may be an unpublished version even—a section in which his most immediate literary friends figure in comical ways, and somebody appears there as the Sun Poet of Estevan. [laughter]

RB: Sun Poet! Ah, Cooley, you are a sun god, we knew it!

TB: How then is a prairie poet defined? We sat in the bar a while ago and we studied Birk Sproxton's poem, *Headframe*: And I said to you at one point, "Finally some sunlight came into the poem." Or something happened in the poem where I thought, oh, finally I'm back on the prairie! I sensed something in there that brought me back to the prairies.

DC: You know one thing I think that happens in a lot of those texts is a strong sense of culture building, of building from the roots up. In a lot of those long prairie poems we're starting here and we're finding ways of writing ambitious texts out of the prairies. I think a lot of those poems carry those marks in one way or another.

RB: And so then the prairie poem becomes not so much something innate in the prairies, but a literary tradition that's built on these poems, poems that are imitating Robert Kroetsch's *Seed Catalogue*, building on a specific literary tradition, all these things that are emulated.

TB: It's interesting what you say, because I was taught that *Seed Catalogue* was a prairie poem, *Marsh Burning* was a prairie poem—so that when those things come back to me, whatever happens in another poem that relates me back to those poems, I sense prairie. It's about learning what is a prairie poem, too, right?

DC: Yeah, yeah. When I think about *Marsh Burning* it's nothing but water! I remember when I first met Arnason, comparing notes, there we are in the English department, two boys from the prairies, and I spoke of my world of sun and heat and Arnason spoke of water and fish and boats—I knew he was a fraud then. [laughter]

RB: One of the things I'm learning too, though, is that articulation of prairie poetry, because it's kind of a line of literary models, can be quite exclusive, too. There's a lot of experience outside that that we're starting to discover, too. So that idea of prairie poetry is probably transforming all the time, with new experiences coming into it.

DC: Yeah, yeah, for sure. One of the interesting things is that very few women on the prairies have written long poems, relatively speaking. But, in fact they were! What you get is a kind of long poem that isn't getting attended to very well, a kind of cycle of related lyrics; you get a lot of those from women. I would argue you've got a serial long poem there, or at least you've got text that can be read in such a way. But it hasn't been.

RB: There are lots of people who come to the prairies and are re-articulating the prairie experience from all sorts of angles. I'm just reading Uma Parameswaran's book *Trishanku*, which is a beautiful articulation of the confluence of the Assiniboine and Red, and the Ganga in India, how those two traditions blend. It's a wonderful prairie poem. There are fifteen different voices in this poem—a traditional prairie long poem? I think so. So, does the long poem come out of theoretical kinds of consideration? Maybe with Bakhtin?

DC: Bakhtin actually enters a little later than those first ones. I can actually remember—I can't give you the date, but I can exactly remember when it entered my world. It was when I had written most of what became part of *Bloody Jack*, well into it, and Kroetsch had been off at some conference and had heard a paper, found a book or whatever, and he said, "I've found something really interesting, Cooley, I'll send it to you." A couple of days later come two xeroxed chapters of Bakhtin. This is what I'm doing! So that would be about '82 or '83 or something like that.

TB: I think you're probably answering the question already, but I just want to push it a bit—does your understanding of theory influence your poetry?

DC: Well, you internalize a lot of those things. Here we are talking English. About as unnatural as you can get. Right? It's an utterly artificial construction. But we have so internalized it and its conventions that it's second nature to us. But it's no "natural." Obviously it looks like the capacity to enter speech is natural to the species, but the speech we enter, learn, that informs our thinking and experience, is totally an artificial construction. We internalize its rules, its patterns.

TB: But you get away with it in your poetry. Have you heard back from an editor saying, "This is too theoretical, or too meta-lingual, or too…" Do they pick up on that?

DC: Yeah. When I was working on *Sunfall*, one of the editors, who is very sympathetic, began to write indignant notes about some of the rhymes that I had. I had a poem that rhymes fair and furls and unfurls and fears and he started writing in the margins "Stop it!" [laughter] That impatience that some people have with language that goes out of its way to acknowledge hanky-panky with other words, words playing with words.

RB: It scares people that a writer would structure a poem around sound rather than meaning.

TB: Any structure, sound or space. What principles do follow concerning the reader's eye?

DC: Part of it is, I hate a kind of lumpy proportion on the page, so I sometimes choose to run things just in a thin line down the left margin, but generally not, especially if for various reasons I want a shorter line inside of longer lines. I hate the look of one single word all by itself on a line against longer lines; it seems really awkward and ungracious. The dispersal of words in a poem for me partly involves a sense of grace, gracefulness.

RB: When I read your poetry I see you very carefully balancing semantic weights so that one word on a line, unless it's a pretty heavy word, can't carry the weight of the line. Same with your space, the meaningful weight of space.

TB: You play with splitting the line and meaning, the visual and then the play of multiple meanings.

DC: Yeah, and that upsets a lot of people. There is a real sense of "fit," a niceness, to a line whose syntactic or grammatical unit and semantic unit coincide. Especially ones that are quiet or more tender. And if you break that, there's a real sense of violation in many ways, and readers can even feel betrayal. In fact, I tend not to do it as much in the quieter poems. You just come to a kind of rest here, in a poem that's fairly quiet, and you say, Damn it, it wasn't a rest! In that sense, you do a kind of violence to a total experience, I guess.

RB: It has to do with convention, too. That line break is supposed to be a rest in a conventional poem and contain a conventional syntactical unit. Also I think one of the upsetting things is that ambiguity across the line break. It makes the reader go back to the beginning of the line, and as readers, we don't necessarily want to go back. Most readers. Same with the pun. A pun makes you double back; you've got two things going on at once. It makes you almost stop, you have to go back and think about the other possibility. If you're looking for a clear, singular message, you don't want to have to be going back and forth.

DC: I don't know if you remember a poem called "a poem for the other wise."

<pre>
        they know   exactly
                where   to draw the line
        the line they insist upon

                        a strange sense of letters
                            : she wishes
        you'd "stop   this playing
    around"

                            this getting out
                of line   this being ir
                    responsible foot
            loose &   fancy/free
</pre>

Dedications

"Stop this playing around" is an exact quotation from someone. And that's part of it too. There is often a sense that the poem is supposed to be a site of solemnity and a poet is supposed to be sensitive and well-spoken, right? And a lot of people are scandalized! Here's a poet who's just joking around! This is intolerable! And god knows I do it, too. I write quite traditional poems in many ways. [pause] I've often argued that all poems are love poems.

TB: I've heard you say that before, but—and you often accuse me of being obfuscatory—but, it's very obfuscatory [laughter] because you stop there. And I think it's a very gentle stop, and I think we all nod our heads and go, hmmmmmmm, yeah. And I think we all think we understand it, but I am not sure I do. What does "love" mean in that context?

DC: Well, it's ambiguous enough to cover a lot of ground. [laughter] The first meaning is the traditional one; every poem you write is written to someone or about someone. Another is the love of language. There's even the love of, I suppose, the potential reader, that in certain ways you write something hoping that it's going to connect for someone. I really hope this matters to you, and it connects for you, and will reach you and speak to you in some way. Which is a kind of giving, right?

RB: One of the things I find in your poems, they're chock full of bodies. Especially your body, the male body, in a way I've learned a lot from by emulating. When I first started reading your poetry, I was searching for that alternative model of the male body in writing. And I often think about it now, reading feminist poetry expressing the female body, female desire, and recognizing too that we need to re-express the male body. And so I was relieved to discover your body in poems. Because it is a gentle body, a tender body—

DC: An embarrassing body. [laughter]

RB: A lot of things the traditional male body was not allowed to be. And so that discovery was quite an awakening and really helped me as a young man.

DC: What occurred to me too is that the images would be of smell, of tactility, of fine hairs, of colourings, smalls of necks. But I think there are a lot of love poems in the sexual sense as well as other senses.

RB: And even subtler, I think you write out of a sense of body in terms of the sound, throat, breath, those things that covertly are your body entering the poem.

DC: Breath is there probably as much as sun.

TB: Before the interview, when I said the word "sun" to Rob, he said the word "breath" to me. The way the body is represented is the way the poetry moves away from conventional structures, too. It seems to me that the body moves in the space of the poem in a freedom that the body would not otherwise be given—I mean, the right-hand margin, the couplets, the stanzas, the four, four, four, four—to move away from that is to let the body into the poem.

RB: Or revised by it. I read traditional poetics as being also representations of the body. I think about the solemn body, the structured body, the composed body, all those sorts of things you are revising, giving me another model for body in writing, saying, that's allowed too, we can be that too. There can be that vulnerability. I wasn't really thinking of bodies until the poem in *Sunfall*, "at night cooley listens":

> pain the body moans
> death cooley wails
> they could be into the blues
> cooley tearful the body might leave him
>
> they try to make up once more
> the two of them making sorrow
> full music talking
> it over, intimately, all night long

Sunfall

– 119 –

When I heard that poem I went back and thought—wow, this has been there all along. Here most obviously, but also from the early stages of your writing.

TB: If there's a body, there's always an "other," there's always a binary on the body; it might be God, it might be language, it might be a platonic ideal, it might be something that is not part of the body. In your poetry—I am not talking about your personal life, but in your poetry—what might the "other" be? I think there is God in some sense—

DC: No, I don't think so—I mean, not as in transcendent. How does one name anything? But I don't think that there's a spiritual figure or force outside the material world.

TB: We're sure there's a body in the poem, we're not sure that there's—

DC: Or a coding of the body.

TB: A coding, sure. We're not sure there's a coding of the metaphysical, or the unknown.

DC: There is a strong sense, in many of those texts, of absence, explicit in some of them. I think one of the tonal refrains that runs through a lot of those texts is the sense of absence. Most obviously, I guess, in the poems of death, where you pretty dramatically, acutely realize that.

RB: Also loss—even loss in language? Lack in language?

DC: Yeah, yeah. That may be even a better term than loss: lack. It strikes me as being responsive and it surprises me again.

TB: The "other" might be language in the poems. In the poems where there is an object of desire, or an "other," it may or may not be someone, but it's always language, right?

DC: Well, it's certainly always articulated through language.

TB: So in that way, then, the "other" is language.

DC: Yeah, I am sure you are right.

TB: You're playing with us. [laughter]

DC: I am sure you are right. I get bewildered with linguistic paradoxes, I get lost, and my brain seizes up. [laughter] As soon as anything sounds vaguely Heideggerian, [laughter] I have a mental seizure. [laughter-filled back and forth re: Heidegger]

RB: What are you reading now? I know when you are teaching you have a lot of things to draw on in your teaching, but sometimes I wonder about what you are reading on the side that you don't pass on.

DC: I was reading a bunch of theory of travel writing and document. I've been interested in document for a long time and have started to become more interested in travel writing in the last couple years, and I'm increasingly moving into the territory that people would name "postcolonial."

RB: And that informed *Passwords*?

DC: Yeah. I had started reading stuff about travel writing, the theory of travel writing, so I think a little bit of it leaked into there at the very end, as I was just about done. So one of the projects I'm working on is to read a series of four or five or six Canadian travel journals, and to theorize in particular how the "I" is positioned, as much as there is one, how that figure is positioned, especially linguistically and deictically. How they are marked. I've got this notion that in Canadian texts those figures are not going to be speaking in language that would suggest that they find the world disappointing. I think that the Canadian traveler, especially the Canadian postmodern traveler, is not someone who would bring the world to an accounting.

RB: So Frank Davey's *The Abbotsford Guide to India*?

DC: Yeah, that's one of them. Though he's the one who's most obviously semiotic in his text. The ones I'm looking at right now are that one, P.K. Page's *Brazilian Journal*, Daphne Marlatt's *Zócalo*, and Mandel's *Life Sentence* or *Out of Place*, those ones especially. And I'm probably going to get a couple more, like Karen Connelly's journal, which looks to me like a very different kind of journal.

RB: And of course every time I walk into your office, you're reading another book of poetry. Recently, what poetry that has come out has excited you? Last time I was in you were reading some George Elliott Clarke—

DC: Oh yeah, yeah!

[apparently some difficulty with the tape recorder, the distinct sound of beer sloshing everywhere]

TB: We're fine! We're fine! Everyone just relax! [laughter]

RB: The poetics of spilling a draft. What essays on Dennis Cooley's poetry get to the issues that should be addressed?

DC: Debbie Keahey's essay is a terrific essay, the one she wrote a few years ago—her typical Keahey shrewdness and sensitivity and elegance, sophistication. Andrew Stubbs has written something that works off a kind of deconstructive Freudianism, and all sorts of oxymoronic, paradoxical statements. I was really pleased and excited, I mean, the intelligence and the care and the thoughtfulness he had given it just overwhelmed me. I can't understand most of it, [laughs] but I was really impressed and grateful.

RB: Last question?

TB: I've got one that I haven't asked yet. What pisses you off?

DC: You know, I'd answer that in quite a different sense maybe, but meanness and mean-spiritedness probably appalls me more than anything else. It bewilders me. How could anybody have killed Christ? How could they have done that? I don't mean that anger or even hatred piss me off or that I find them incomprehensible. I'm making a distinction here. Meanness as in going out of one's way to hurt somebody.

TB: I'm truly moved by the way you respond. I think you are very genuinely upset that people don't treat one another as human beings, for God's sake. And there are so few people who have the ability to be congruent with the way they feel and speak, and one of the things you have is that, and I wanted to put that on the record.

RB: In your teaching and in your poetry, that gentleness.

DC: Cooley dreams his way into the world hoping for goodness and finding it much of the time, but I'm always reeling, you know, you get smacked and you see other people getting smacked, and ohhh! you know? Two of the greatest lines ever written, Leonard Cohen: "The children are leaning out for love/and they will lean that way forever."

Robert Kroetsch & Dawne McCance:

Different Ways to Keep Warm in the World
Or, I Wanted to Do an Interview

RK: "…tomorrow, and tomorrow, and tomorrow, creeps in this petty pace from day to day…"

RB: We three are in Winnipeg and it's cold enough to freeze…

　　　　　　　　　　　　　　　　　　　…the balls off a brass monkey

RK:　　　　　　　　　　　　　　　…the nuts off an iron bridge.

RB: I am going to read a passage from "Letters to Salonika": "Time rewrites every book. We try so to construct a book/that time, rewriting, will make it better."

A couple years ago Robert Kroetsch renounced writing poetry—a couple years ago? What, 1992? Earlier? And when you did this I was aghast, I was a grad student at the University of Manitoba and we were sitting in Merk's pub (which was formerly Shakey's) on Pembina, and when thinking about it recently I couldn't help think of the pop star Prince who, in order to get out of a recording contract with a company he claimed used him as "slave labour," recorded an album under the name of a visual symbol and announcers would refer to the album as by the "artist formerly known as Prince." And here we have Bob Kroetsch, a writer formerly known as poet. What has become of that renunciation?

RK: Well, I do have a book of poems now, *The Hornbooks of Rita K.* I got around it in a certain way; I invented a woman poet who, even though I had quit, continued to write.

"The question is always a question of trace. What remains of what does not remain?"

The Hornbooks of Rita K

I have decided to renounce the writing of poetry and to devote my life during the remaining decade of an appalling century to an examination of the notebooks and manuscripts of Rita Kleinhart, the brilliant poet who disappeared on June 26, 1992, at the age of fifty-five. A recluse by nature, she apparently traveled outside Canada only once; she gave only three public readings; she lectured twice to academic audiences. And of course she published the ninety-eight brief poems (hornbooks she chose to call them; somewhat pretentiously, it seems to me) that are the basis of her quiet yet enduring reputation.

"The Poetics of Rita K"

RB: Even before Rita Kleinhart you had found ways of getting out of being the owner of the poem or the unified centre of the poem and instead created a representation field devoid of authorial authority. You escape.

RK: I suppose I did. I wasn't aware of it at the time but I do get restless with the "I" in so many poems and I am certainly resistant to the unified centre. But I end up inventing a woman who is a certain part of myself obviously.

RB: This idea of the lyrical "I" is thrown around in poetic discussions—a poet is either a supporter of the lyric or working against it. How would you articulate that tension in contemporary poetics?

RK: That's a central question in poetry I think. I think about your own work—to turn it around—you resist the lyric "I," am I right? So, how do you think of the lyric "I"?

RB: Part of what I'm seeing...again I am going to shift it away...a lot of the writers I respect in Canada now have a problem with the lyric "I" because it has a loaded history in terms of race or gender or sexuality, where that lyric because of the history of literature has come to represent something that, to survive, these writers have to disavow. When you have a lyric "I" there is a belief in presence. A speaker behind the text, they are there, present.

RK: Each of us is many voices. That's why I distrust the authority of that lyric "I." Sort of forgoes one's own multiplicity. So look for a way to let the multiplicity speak itself and then that has consequences. You lose a sense of centredness.

RB: In terms of text and writing or in terms of life?

RK: Wow, well, I think poetry carries over into life or poetry comes out of life. I certainly don't separate the two. In fact, there's less and less room for separation. Poetry instructs us.

> I AM/naught. That's all I is. Mmmmmmmmmmmm.
>
> Zzzzzzzzzzzzzzzzz.
>
> The first time our mouths opened and our tongues ran hot and wet in their impossible wish to exchange places ( )
>
> The first time the voice said huh-uh—
>
> "After Paradise"

DM: To say that there is no easy separation between poetry and life, there is a problem there...through the lyric "I," can we locate a life in a work?

RK: The poet has a body and has a history but both are very problematic.

DM: What do you mean by problematic?

RK: Well, what is my history? What is one's history? I often think of the little film they did about my past and we shot for maybe forty or fifty hours and put out a half-hour film. So you realize what that filmmaker could have done, the different lives he could have constructed for me. It's the same with a body in a certain way. Yesterday I was very exhausted for some reason and I would have said different things in this interview. This morning I've been waiting for Rob to arrive. I thought it was kind of ironic that the furnace man and the poet arrived on the same morning. Different ways to keep warm in the world. One has a very different body on certain days.

> June 26
>
> THE POET, ALONE, ON HIS 54TH BIRTHDAY, REFLECTS ON HIS 54TH BIRTHDAY.
>
> "Letters to Salonika"

RB: And Rita's body?

RK: Yeah, OK. I keep her body very ambiguous. When I was writing I was thinking should I describe her, how tall is she, but that's not what it's about. Her body is something else. I guess it's a part of our cultural investigation of "the body."

RB: One way to think about it is the connection between poetics and the struggle over identity. Your poems are fragmented into various voices or move very quickly between different speech acts and that poetics leads to something.

RK: One is interested in how a reader enters a text. This fragmenting leaves lots of gaps where the reader can come in and participate. As opposed to the unified speaker—the reader is so much a listener, not a participant.

> "fragment after a fragment." That would be my title for her work. I once wrote to Rita, telling her as much.
>
> *The Hornbooks of Rita K*
>
> The track of the swallow is certain but unpredictable.
> Dismembered, the poem assures itself: hold on there.
>
> "The Poetics of Rita K"

RB: Students tend to resist the idea of participating and typically come up against your texts after coming from a tradition of reading that disallows their entrance into poems. What do you say to them when they come upon a poem like "Seed Catalogue"? What would you tell them to give them a hand into your poems?

RK: Let yourself do it. Don't let an inherited way of reading come between you and the text. You have to engage the text. I guess that's it—you have to let yourself experience the text and that means allowing surprise, discomfort, revelation, boredom, whatever.

RB: That's a very open uncoded process but could you argue that the postmodern text just has different codes by which it functions, like how to read the text, just another code of reading?

RK: In a certain way, it is another code of reading but it's a code that says, be a vulnerable reader, let yourself be vulnerable, be exposed. A lot of poetry keeps the poet safe and the reader safe. Granted, posmodernism is another code, sometimes a bad one. But you say to a reader: I am taking a risk, share my risk.

RB: Taking risks with language.

RK: Yes! That's the most exciting thing of all. I mean that's *really* taking a risk—taking a risk with language.

If I understand you correctly you are saying that you

Catastrophe is a shade of blue. Or is it merely the name of a
perfume that once

The crispness of the celery, so to speak, somehow reminded me

The distortion of the poem by the image is endemic to analysis,
or at least your analysis suggests

If your heart isn't in it, why eat the goulash, comma

"Revisions of Letters Already Sent"

RB: Because the way language is bound up with self, it becomes amplified. So
you are a daredevil.

DM: It might have something to do with materiality too, would you agree
with that? In the sense that you can't easily read from a distance, there is a
kind of work of reading, one text leads you to another text. There is more of
a tangle that sustains. This is what I find with Rita Kleinhart—you can't stay
away from it in a safe place—you have to start working with it.

RB: When I read the hornbooks, I couldn't help but think of a kind of
high-wire act.

RK: That's ironic, I was thinking of your interest in the circus. I am sure when
you were working on the idea of the circus you were thinking of it as a kind
of metaphoric exploration of writing.

RB: In the sense of performance and audience. What I was really thinking
about, and it's interesting to think about in terms of your poetry, was a sense of
what does "free space" mean? It's what I was talking about, getting away from
a kind of coded tradition of poetry—into what? A free space? Probably not.
Now, postmodern codes are not necessarily a bad thing. Going back to when
I first started reading your poetry. Everybody said, read Bakhtin. And there were
all sorts of things happening in between your work and his. But then I got
frustrated and suspicious with Bakhtin's notion of the carnivalesque as being
free space. We have to learn to read in a transition space—it is free space
because it is as yet uncoded. We start reading poetry in connection to Pynchon
or Stein. How do we start making generalizations about what's going on? The
temptation in an interview like this one is to start naming it: okay, what's going
on here? Terms like multiplicity, deferral; these words that then say we have
mastery over the text. These generalizations, this mastery, is not free space.

Carnival laughter is the laughter of all the people. Second, it is universal in scope; it is directed at all and everyone, including the carnival's participants. The entire world is seen in its droll aspect, in its gay relativity. Third, this laughter is ambivalent: it is gay, triumphant, and at the same time mocking, deriding. It asserts and denies, it buries and revives.

Mikhail Bakhtin, *Rabelais and His World*

RK: It's useful seeing the poet as being on a wire without a net. You look at physics—the idea of indeterminacy is over 100 years old. The sense of indeterminacy—what I marvel at is how long it took poets to see it! You can say that ten people out of 1000 are going to get the flu but you can't say which ten it will be. Poetry acknowledges this indeterminacy—it calls into question logic, a kind of cause and effect that has been given too much authority.

RB: Along with assumptions of a unified subject or assumptions of language function. One of the ways I was thinking about it yesterday as I was reading texts that are very political: how could you see poetry as a type of governance? As a way of articulating a kind of communal guidance?

RK: Being so political...

DM: I have some questions along the way, one of them being: what are we calling poetry? To re-address the lyric "I" seems to me to have to do something with genre—your writing always crosses genre boundaries. Look at Rita Kleinhart: you have to ask—what makes this poetry? This crossing is one way that I think your writing connects to the political, rather than through some kind of dictum—you connect through the form of your work. I wonder why you call Rita Kleinhart poetry?

RB: He didn't originally. I remember approaching him and saying "This is poetry!" and him saying "No, no, no."

RK: It did become a political issue for me. I'm fascinated by our sense of the communal, people interacting. In Rita Kleinhart, I have three people interacting: Rita, the critic Raymond and a guy named Robert who appears once in while as a kind of incompetent friend. It was the notion of the lyric that gave us such a narrow definition to poetry. I think you're right, we have to cross genre boundaries. You've done it emphatically.

RB: And so that tradition of the lyric, if we go along with the governance idea, would be autocratic, a tyranny, a dictatorship. So in some ways this is revolutionary, a new governance that functions on certain more democratic principles. So, when you are inviting the reader to participate you are creating a more democratic process.

RK: But you were saying that every year students are farther away from poetry. I don't think it is the fault of the students, I think it's the fault of poetry. Poetry has failed. It's like the NDP—we all admire its principles, but it's not connecting with the world. And poetry is not connecting. When I sent the hornbooks to the editor, she said, "I can really get into this." That's the highest compliment she can pay me. Poetry has, almost proudly, refused to let you in for many reasons. One was a modernist posture. Eliot and Pound said you have to be difficult. Or you have to be confessional, private but shamelessly public. We've been trying to find a connection. I think the people who are writing political poetry are trying desperately to make poetry matter.

RB: One of the things that happens in books of poetry is that you teach the reader how to read, because you have them there, indicating what is needed from the reader. It is hard to work against all the ways we are taught not to respond.

RK: Like getting pissed off. Yeah.

RB: What about the poetic novel? In some ways the boundary between the novel and the long poem has nearly dissolved. Is that fair to say? Novels coming out now read as long poems? As a writer, I might be searching for that middle ground. You have to admire someone like Michael Ondaatje, who has moved in his aesthetic sensibility. I used to think he betrayed his sensibilities. Now I wonder. Either you write a *Collected Works of Billy the Kid* and 300 people read it and you are making a statement about identity and language and form but probably speaking to the converted, or you write *In the Skin of a Lion*, which many more people will read but has that different aesthetic.

DM: These are issues of readership.

RK: People seem anxious the minute they see broken lines. The visual of the broken line meets a lot of resistance. People will read very dense poetic passages by Ondaatje and not feel threatened by them. Ironically, in a certain way I feel your poetry is more accessible than your novel. It's the consolation of prose—they say, "I can deal with this."

RB: I have come to say I will trick people into reading poetry by abandoning the line.

DM: I can't follow here. I thought we started off with students resisting poetry, so now we're talking about a larger readership that prose attracts.

RB: The question is—what would happen if we abandoned poetry?

RK: It was in the '80s, actually, that I announced I was finished with poetry. In a way, I was abandoning a definition of poetry. The thing that intrigues me is that I spent eight years working on Rita—that certainly undoes the lyric moment. If you took a moment of ecstasy or recognition and dwelt on it for eight years—it has to become something else. One thing that it becomes is a kind of narrative, or a meditation, or a different kind of fragment. The fragment is what you are interested in.

RB: The way a fragment resists linear narrative. I have been thinking about the word *mastery*—how can you create a text that does not claim any sort of mastery. Your "found" poetry does that in some way—you are a collector, not a formulated a grand vision.

RK: Dawne published a chapbook called *etymologies of dawne* that is a sort of collection of quotes. Defend that. You as poet exist only in the blanks between quotes.

DM: I was thinking of a number of things there. I would go to your interest in the connection between poetry and theory, to not disconnecting them in a radical way. Most of the quotes are theoretical or philosophical. I am interested in the form of this kind of writing, too. There is a lot of poetic writing in contemporary theory. I have a hard time reading Kroetsch's poetry as outside of such theory. I am interested in reading Rita Kleinhart this way. Under the name of Robert Kroetsch, we do not, in Rita, find an author so much as a network of other texts: this is one way that, in reading Rita, we come to a discovery of absence; we never locate a mastering figure, an autobiographical "I."

> Kristeva: Unlike "the white of dazzling light, a transparent light of meaning cut off from the body," the blue expanse of Giotto's Padua frescoes energies, "eroticiz[es] the body proper."

> Rhythm/interval/gesture: Matisse speaks of color's physiological effect, trembling/quiver, a borderline "*retinal sensation* [that] destroys the calm of the surface and the contour," a "*tactile vitality*" that is comparable to "the vibrato" of voice and hearing.

"empty chairs suspended in a blue expanse"
no self here to find, no proper name

etymologies of dawne

HORNBOOK #30

Why do I imagine phone calls in which she tells me I have
disappeared?

The Hornbooks of Rita K

RB: And the same thing in your book?

DM: I was trying to play with a loss that is located, in some way, in my
life. And I was trying to discover a form through a kind of conversation
between texts.

RB: The idea of a generative form—each time a poem is written it has to be…

DM: You write after something that is no longer waiting/there for you. I'm
not sure where writing actually begins or if it ends. But I think it is a way for
us to ask questions.

And since the fovea, with its centered vision,
is that part of the eye developed latest in human beings (about sixteen months
after birth, at the time of the mirror stage, when the would-be subject
first identifies its self with an idealized image of its own
form), the "noncentered or decentering effect" of blue extends not only to
objects but to the specular "I" as well.

etymologies of dawne

RK: Is the autobiographical a way to ask questions?

DM: I think so. We are interested in this problem of authorship and in
autobiographical writing that, as is the case with Rita, works free of
authorial claims.

RK: The idea of using another text, collecting, is resisting
the autobiographical.

DM: It is and it isn't. I suppose that critical writing is not supposed to belong
to autobiography, a point that puzzles and interests me.

"an excess of names, a more-than-name become space and color."

etymologies of dawne

RK: I wonder to what extent this book, *In Muddy Water*, is an autobiography of Rob.

RB: The book is almost a mapping of who I based my poetics on. When I was sketching out questions, I wanted to talk about a lot of things that aren't interview material: the course we were in, where I came from... I have been thinking of how I am constructed as a poet. Where did this come from, where did my ideas about form come from? You say the form is not waiting for us to enter but we do assume forms like a pose. Where do we learn those muscles? I think about pictures on the back of poetry books. I think about the picture on your disOrientation chapbook—you with this big face and mouth grinning madly.

RK: My recollection of you in the course is visual. Standing back and coming forward ambiguously, undecided. But a physical presence. That's good that we are physical.

RB: I remember you saying nothing, refusing to tell us anything. I find that in my students too—they want me to say something.

RK: If you tell them something they will never remember, let them say it and they'll remember forever. Dawne McCance is famous for that.

DM: You are too.

RB: It's hard work. Hard work not saying anything. Because that's the easiest thing to do—to say something. It's work for us not to say anything here in this interview.

RK: But, I think it's good that *In Muddy Water* has your signature all over the place.

RB: As collector, yeah. One of the things I was considering heading into this was *Labyrinths of Voice*. That text turned me on to all sorts of things—the way you cluttered it up with texts and that network of reading. To be able to network out from this to other texts, Derrida, Calvino, writers I may not have discovered. Interview as matchmaker. What would you say to a student or reader who had *Completed Field Notes* or *The Hornbooks of Rita K*—what other texts would you put in their hands?

RK: Dennis Cooley's *Bloody Jack*.

> now
> the new snow brightens
> my window deepens
> lays its light
> upon the ground
> the grass below
> that holds it gasgreen
> into the yellow warmth
> in early November

Bloody Jack

I think I read you, Rob, before you write your book. William Carlos Williams. Not necessarily another long poem. Ezra Pound, a few of his poems. A creative writing class will produce a text, a context. Students reading one another, writing in response to one another. Every class is so different. They are producing a text.

RB: I remember you getting mad at us for writing "autumn poems."

RK: Right, I remember too. We don't write about autumn, we write about fall. We have fall here and not very much of it. Winter starts today, as I understand, and we've had a month of fierce cold. Tell me about autumn!

RB: But the autumn poem was default and you woke us up. The weight of the tradition leads us to autumn poems and that leads us to write about the imprint of not-here.

RK: Right, you're not in Renaissance England and you're not in Basho's Japan; you're right here. You're here, now tell me about it.

> the absence of silkworms
> the absence of clay and wattles (whatever the hell
> they are)
> the absence of Lord Nelson
> the absence of kings and queens
> the absence of a bottle opener, and me with a vicious
> attack of the 26-ounce flu

Seed Catalogue

RB: In that imaginative world, many writers are still writing about "there." Students land on the local element—that this was about here, this is located, named as here, the prairies, the Battle River…

RK: You don't know how many people have come up to me and picked out my mention of the High Level Bridge in *The Studhorse Man*. The High Level Bridge. That's our life, our bridge, not the London Bridge or wherever.

> The Nairn Overpass has been under repair since before it was
> completed. Railway engineers, passing beneath its uncertain arch,
> speak wisely of the decline of empires. One of the winos who
> sleeps in its shade has added a sundeck to his shopping bags.
>
> "After Paradise"

RB: But it's so engrained. I'll ask a creative writing class to write something about Winnipeg and they refuse. They say there's nothing to write about. Nothing story-worthy. It's cold and snow; it's a big obstacle. And here there are sphinxes on the legislative building—sphinxes! —now what on earth are they doing there? What do they have to do with experience of the prairie?

DM: I like to read poetry as a kind of architecture. If you are going to frustrate the lyric "I," to open the point of presence, some interesting things have to happen—in a very material way—on the page and throughout the text, one space giving over to another. I think these issues of form and movement make writing and reading a lot of fun.

RK: Like a drive to work. Rob, you drive an hour to the city. Just imagine going for an hour every day through that space. It would give you a very different sense of the world than a drive down Pembina. I bet every drive is a little different. For me it's space that's important.

RB: Especially when I drive past the end of the prairies. It connects for me with your metaphor of the "field" (is it a metaphor? allegory?) and I talk about it to my students as a type of reading act, moving through a space not on a path. You have these ways of moving. The art of the poet is to create that engaging space in which there are many possibilities from movement. Students try a structuralist reading on your poems—trying to gather images, trace repetitions, formulate a pattern. It always fails, whether they know it or not. They're after a sense of the whole poem. When they think of it as many different possible "wholes," that opens it up for them.

DM: The poet creates. I like the idea of "field notes" with its discontinuities and dislocations.

RB: A search or discovery.

RK: When Rob says he lives on the shore of Lake Agassiz, it's literally true. Yet it's quite astonishing to a reader who might say—"come on." You don't really imagine it, you discovered it.

> 3/4/85
> Here on the coast of North Dakota, we pretend against our desire. Over wine and chilled oysters, we touch each other with promises. In the seaweed on the shore of your bed, we smell the cold film of our spent bodies. Which of us wrote the narrative line?

> "Excerpts from the Real World"

RB: And then finding Winnipeg as a kind of Atlantis. It is easy to imagine coming down that slope. Now I am entering water. This idea of space interests me. I may have it wrong, but Octavio Paz conceives of architecture as an artificial space and literature/writing as an artificial time. But poetry, especially long poems, has less to do with artificial time than more narrative forms. Don't you think?

DM: I am willing to concede that time is not presence but space and spacing.

RB: Is architecture about time then?

DM: One of the interesting things that is going on in architecture is exploration of the conjunction of idea and form. How to give form to some of the things you've been talking about today is a lively activity in architecture. I don't really see much difference between one kind of representation and another. I like to think of the text as a text.

RB: I like the idea of collapsing the distinction between different types of texts. I wonder more about what the premise was for dividing up the types of form into genre. It's hard for me not to think about form in terms of power: certain divisions and certain forms as inscriptions of power. A form then has a certain status and its maintenance becomes a matter of maintaining power.

RK: One of the reasons poetry hasn't changed is because it wants to hold onto the power that the tradition has announced. The irony is that the attempt to hold onto that power has made poetry powerless, more and more irrelevant. You end up with a paradox: you have to give up the power to get it.

DM: What is interesting about poetry and architecture today is their parallel discovery or allowance of a system of discontinuities. They have affinities with each other. But, Robert, you are doing something in Rita that is very much related to power.

RB: Is postmodern aesthetics a type of power?

DM: It's not outside of power. Whether it consolidates or dislocates depends on what it is doing.

RB: In academic institutions, there is a sense of mastery over discourses. Academic discourse has become a site where claims are made of mastery. There is a naming, a categorization, a translation, a reduction, I would say, for academic purposes. Not for the well-being of people. I wonder if there is the same sort of layering in postmodern thought where you get postmodern writing or art, then you have a postmodern discourse that works against the very things that movement espouses.

RK: The postmodern resists hierarchies, so you have to knock down the primacy of poetry, for example. By naming it as postmodern you resume a kind of power. I guess to name is at once to gain some power and to lose some power. Once you name something, you have a little bit of control over it, going back to Genesis once again. But once you name it you've lost something, you've fossilized yourself.

RB: In certain environments, that kind of naming holds a lot of currency.

RK: Certainly, "postcolonial," for example. It's so fluid and complex.

RB: In A *Likely Story*, reading "I Wanted to Write a Manifesto," one would be tempted, in your position, to write an essay on the postmodern occasion or something but you resist that through the "out" of autobiography, or you escape into autobiography. Which I admire, because I think you do sidestep some of the issues we've been talking about. I am imagining that the pressure on you even in this interview to be authoritative is immense.

RK: The anecdote is so interesting as a sidestepping. The anecdote resists the pronouncement.

RB: You make connections between writing and sexuality, but you are not naming or theorizing that connection in such a way that it becomes pronouncement.

RK: When I say, "I Wanted to Write a Manifesto," there is an implication that I didn't. Maybe I did. And I did, and didn't. Leaving the gate open for myself. I've been accused of that all the time.

DM: I just taught a course on "haunting." In your writing, Robert, I like the idea, not of "sidestepping," avoiding, but of stepping to the side with something that continues to provoke, that persists...you can't stop the spectrality or the haunting effect.

RK: We live in Muddy Water as opposed to Clear Water. There is something there but you only get signals, you see a ripple. I think Muddy Water is a little more interesting than Clear Water. It's exciting, it's dangerous, it's full of possibility. It is a kind of haunted landscape, or waterscape.

Jon Paul Fiorentino:

Secrets and Creaking Hinges

RB: So I am gathering from you a kind of postmodern affinity to practices of indeterminacy and uncertainty. Would you describe (vs. prescribe) your poetry as "postmodern" or a type of "deconstruction"? What orders or hierarchies do you find yourself most wanting to dis-assemble?

JPF: I'm not sure if my poetry is postmodern. It can certainly be read as postmodern and this is what I like about the notion of indeterminacy. There are some poems in the "montreal poems" section of *hover* that I read as very traditional. The discursive rants of "introducing the real" come closest to a kind of deconstruction and it involves gender. I am very interested in the hierarchies of gender and fascinated by gender theory—especially Judith Butler's. I like the idea of dis-assembling through dissembling. By being disobedient and strategically "dishonest" in verse, one can reveal the lack of truth (indeterminacy, uncertainty) in all language—specifically the language that surrounds, suffocates gender.

RB: I've heard you call your poetry "language-based." How does this coincide/interact with "lyricism"? How did you arrive at the term "language-based"?

JPF: If I arrived at that term in the past it was probably because it was thrust upon me. I was accused by certain conservative types in Montreal of being a "language poet," as if that is some kind of pejorative. "Language-based" is an obvious label for any poet—all poetry is language-based. Perhaps language-obsessed is a better description of my poetics.

In some poems I address language as the object of desire; in these texts language becomes the lyric "you." Lyric language is language engaging the "self" in the most accessible sense and in the most philosophical Lacanian sense. It is language engaging the semantics of "self" by addressing the "other." It is interesting to think of language as the "other" in this dialectic. I am drawn to semantic possibilities, to alternate ways of meaning.

> i never got a chance to stray
>
> > that is to say we never got a chance
>
> > to stray from our bodies
>
> > > > "lyric 3"

Poets like Nicole Brossard fascinate me. She has taken her desire for language to some strange places.

RB: Why do you think "language-based" or "language-obsessed" poetry scares the conservatives? There is this political aspect of poetry, where there are factions and camps and power centres—but how else would you describe your poetry as political? I remember in a theory class you scoffing at my suggestion that all language acts are political. Do you still scoff?

JPF: I still scoff, but not at this suggestion. The poetry I admire scares the conservatives because it reveals that language is political and an economy of power. More specifically, poetry can reveal specific linguistic and literary conventions that are designed to exclude. A great deal of literary conservatism aims to exclude through the maintenance of convention.

Language is performative. I am reading J.L. Austin: "it is never a gift if I say 'I give it to you' but never hand it over." Much of traditional literature uses this party trick—offering the reader insight, brilliance, while at the same time denying access to the realm of literature by imposing formal and rigid conventions that exclude any possibility of "otherness."

I understood the phrase "art for art's sake" much more intimately when I realized the inherent political aim of this statement. Walter Pater and Oscar Wilde were endeavouring to find a way for literature to allow alternate poetics into the exclusive structure of expressive art/theory.

It remains my ultimate hope that I will offer alternate ways of meaning to the reader and at the same time remain open to possibilities outside my subjectivity. In my poetics statement I wrote that I had no interest in being prescriptive. Your assertion that all language acts are political is reinforced by the revelation that my statement is in itself prescriptive.

RB: When you read you perform a kind of sardonic, even antagonistic, drama on stage between poems. How do see that changing the poetry reading event? How does that change/contextualize the poetry?

JPF: I am just trying to keep the audience awake. I think I try to infuse a kind of urgent, tragi-comic personality into my readings. Often, I tell terrible jokes and give away my prescriptions to the audience. I had been searching for ways to exceed the audience's expectations. What I discovered is that an audience generally expects to be bored at a poetry reading. If I can't exceed this expectation than I shouldn't bother reading in front of an audience. I can only assume that the poems are "changed" through my presentation in the sense that the audience isn't in a collective coma and therefore they hear the poem. That's something.

RB: In one of the last lines of *transcona fragments* you describe academia as "incestuous."

> [...] they have taught me to desire each other and so to
> perpetuate an incestuous notion of poetry which is discretely
> referred to as intertextuality.

> write fragments, not full sentences. But most of all disobey all
> instructions toward poetry.

> "prairie long poem"

Tell me more about your relationship with post-secondary institutions and the institutionalized canon.

JPF: I am currently a graduate student and part-time instructor at Concordia University so I am very much a part of the academy. If there is one thing that I am trying to resist in academia, it is the notion of a monolithic, static canon. My tribute to the "Prairie Long Poem" celebrates the texts I discovered as alternative literature, but also acknowledges the canon formation that these texts become a part of. Canon formation is always tinged with incest.

RB: Tell me about consciousness-altering medication and its role in poetry.

JPF: I take many prescriptions. I used to self-medicate a lot as well. All I can say about this is: the real writing occurs during the editing stage and I do believe one should be sober at this stage.

RB: Talk about the difference between the Montreal and Winnipeg writing communities. Who have been important influences/contacts in each city and how did they affect your writing or poetics?

JPF: In Winnipeg, I was lucky enough to study with Robert Budde [pshaw] and Catherine Hunter. I was encouraged and promoted by these two lovely people and I am eternally grateful for that (they are two of my favourite writers as well). I also studied and worked with the poet Chandra Mayor during my time in Winnipeg. She greatly affected the way I look at the role of gender in poetry. She turned me on to Judith Butler; she challenged me to read myself out of gender traps and reductive poetics. In Montreal, I have been lucky enough to work with Mary di Michele, who provides me with a great number of helpful edits and gives me a sense of permission to proceed with the poetic voice I have established—this is so important. I work with Robert Allen at *Matrix* and he is a very cool writer. There are some amazing writers in Montreal like David McGimpsey, Sarah Steinberg, Ryan Arnold, Corey Frost.

RB: What one poem you studied in school influenced you the most? What kind of poetry are you repulsed by?

JPF: "Not Waving but Drowning" by Stevie Smith is still my favourite poem. I'm not sure if I ever studied it in school but I always brought it to class. I am repulsed by simple-minded, Eurocentric, hyper-formalist, hyper-masculine, emulation poetry.

RB: Gender and gender play are an obvious element in your thinking/poetry. Tell me what your poetry does to alter gender fashionings.

JPF: Poetry is about the possibilities of language and my interest is in finding alternate ways of fashioning something. Gender is something: something to play with, to revise, to interrogate. I cannot stand the idea of a prescriptive, binary-based understanding of gender: it is not a fixed biological truth and I hope, by the end of my career as a writer (which should be any day now) I will have performed some interesting gender theory within poetry. Denise Riley, Nicole Brossard, and Daphne Marlatt are a few poets who do it well. I like the notion of poetry-as-theory. It has saved my academic life on more than one occasion.

RB: Your poetics seem hinged around the "I" (including in your articulation of it/them). Tell me the nature of your lyric "I." Is it you?

this is tasteless   i'm stuck in bed
hypergravity
dispensable in pill form
      eyes rolled crossed or shut
shadowing tidal under the dark star's gaze
blinds drawn

"lyric 4.1"

JPF: The creaking hinge that is "I." It is my voice in the sense that it stems from my subjectivity, my perception. I am self-obsessed—perhaps this keeps my "lyric I" close to me. However, it is not me because it is a fictional voice. The "lyric I" relies on its fictional status—it keeps the poetic voice from being truthful. The worst thing a lyric poet can do is tell the truth. Poetry, lyrical or other, is most interesting and engaging when it is deceitful.

Poetry is a process of transmitting secrets to others. Typically I engage in a lyrical mode of writing that attempts to negotiate and revise memory. I am drawn to poets like Emily Dickinson, Adrienne Rich, Sylvia Plath, Nicole Brossard, who are at once personal/confessional/political. Writing poetry is an ideological nightmare. I am lured toward aesthetic idealism; I attempt to inscribe my verse with possibilities; I am wary of insisting on imperatives, and the poetics I desire most challenge moral and cultural imperatives. The challenge lies in not getting trapped by one's own beliefs, assumptions, values. I have no interest in being prescriptive.

RB: You are currently working on a project called "Post-Prairie" with Robert Kroetsch, in which you are collecting new prairie writing that moves away from the rural lyric-based poetics we traditionally associate with the prairies. How are you a post-prairie poet? What do you do that unsettles the canon?

JPF: I don't think the post-prairie aesthetic completely moves away from the past and the rural but it does resituate the "home place" in terms of poetic practice. I would like to think of post-prairie poetics as a descriptive (as opposed to prescriptive) poetics. Many of my poems are urban texts but many of my poems are lyric-based as well. I know the prairie tradition; I have reverence for the prairie tradition; but I am not interested in maintaining that tradition. In my poetry, the traditional prairie is not applicable. The specificity of "my home" is at odds with a canon-friendly home. My home is a place of extreme anxiety, fetishistic language, linguistic music; my home is St. Marc Street in Montreal, Smith Street in Winnipeg. It is always displaced; it is always the "other" place. I think this is the case with more and more poetic voices that have emerged from the prairies. There is a constant revision at work and the author is not always the one revising.

I am interested in those vivid flashes of memory that insist on being recorded—the haunting of classrooms, playgrounds, empty streets (especially streets of Winnipeg). Urban existence fascinates me—swarms of pedestrians, traces of breath at every turn. I am equally fascinated by rhetoric, from the notion of the vernacular muse to the Socratic method. Poetry is a realm of linguistic possibilities, of other ways of asserting one's one existence, of asserting Otherness.

Poetry is equally a realm of sublimated signs. It is important to acknowledge the importance of concealing as much as the importance of revealing. Language is concealment and revelation—the transmission of secrets.

I believe in a poetics of resistance. I assume that poetry can be effective/affective. I value intangible moments of bliss. I enjoy trapping myself in words.

Biographies:

Catherine Hunter

teaches English at the University of Winnipeg.
In addition to her three collections of poetry
(the latest, *Latent Heat*, was winner of the
Manitoba Book of the Year Award), she has
published a spoken word CD and three
mysteries/thrillers, including *In the First
Early Days of My Death* (Signature Editions,
2002). She is also the editor of the Canadian
poetry press The Muses' Company.

Melanie Cameron

was born in Kitchener-Waterloo in 1971. She has lived in North Carolina, Saskatchewan, and California, and has also worked, studied, and travelled in France and Latin America. Melanie began an undergraduate degree at the University of Toronto in 1990, earned her BA in Rhetoric and Professional Writing from the University of Waterloo in 1995, then moved to Winnipeg in 1996, where she completed an MA in English Literature at the University of Manitoba. She continues to live in Winnipeg with her husband, Mark Morton, a nonfiction author. Her book, *Holding the Dark* (The Muses' Company 1999), was shortlisted for the Eileen MacTavish Sykes Award for Best First Book by a Manitoba Writer. Melanie was also shortlisted for the John Hirsch Award for Most Promising Manitoba Writer in both 1999 and 2001. Her second book of poetry, *wake*, is scheduled to be published by The Muses' Company in the fall of 2003.

Melanie is Poetry Co-Editor of *Prairie Fire* magazine, and is currently completing her third book.

George Amabile

has been published in Canada, the USA, Europe, South America, Australia and New Zealand in over one hundred anthologies, magazines, journals and periodicals, including *The Penguin Book of Canadian Verse*, *The New Yorker*, *Harper's*, *American Poetry Review* and *Canadian Poetry Review*. He has edited *The Far Point*, *Northern Light* and has published eight books, the most recent being *Tasting the Dark: New and Selected Poems* (The Muses' Company, 2001) which was a finalist for the Manitoba Book of the Year Award. *The Presence of Fire* won the Canadian Authors Literary Award.

Duncan Mercredi

was born in Misipawistik (Grand Rapids) in 1951. He spent a number of years working in bush camps in northern Manitoba and has eventually ended up working for the Department of Indian and Northern Affairs to pay the bills. Writing, however, remains his passion. The author of several chapbooks and four collections of poetry, *the duke of Windsor—wolf sings the blues* (Pemmican Publications, 1997) being the most recent, Duncan's poetry and fiction has appeared in numerous periodicals, including *Prairie Fire*, *Gatherings*, *Absinthe*, and *CV2*, and collections such as *An Anthology of Canadian Native Literature in English* and *Native Poetry in Canada: A Contemporary Anthology*. A member of the Aboriginal Writers Collective, Duncan won the 2000 CANCOM Ross Charles Award and attended a Screenwriters Workshop at the Banff Centre for the Arts.

Patrick Friesen

formerly of Winnipeg, now lives in Vancouver, teaching at Kwantlen University College. He writes poetry, drama, scripts, songs, text for dance and music, etc. His most recent book of poetry is *the breath you take from the lord* (Harbour Publishing, 2002). In collaboration, Marilyn Lerner, composer/pianist, and Friesen have just released a CD of text and improv piano entitled *Small Rooms* (check the web site: <patrickfriesen.com>). Friesen was short-listed for the Governor General's Award for Poetry in 1997. He was also short-listed for the Dorothy Livesay Award (BC Book Awards) for best book of poetry in BC for *st. mary at main* (The Muses' Company) in 1998. In 1994 his book *Blasphemer's Wheel* (Turnstone Press) won the McNally Robinson Book of the Year award in Manitoba.

Méira Cook

Méira's latest book of poetry is *Toward a Catalogue of Falling*, and a third collection, *Slovenly Love*, is forthcoming this year. She has recently returned to Winnipeg.

Todd Bruce

is a Winnipeg born, Calgary based, award winning poet and bookseller. He has published a trilogy of long poems: *Jiggers*, *Birdman* and *Rhapsody in D*. He has also published one piece of short fiction "Pinch" which he also adapted for CBC as a radio drama. Todd served for several years on the editorial board of Turnstone Press. He is currently revising a fourth poetry manuscript, Frieze, and has just completed his first novel Home Street.

Dennis Cooley

was born in Estevan, Saskatchewan, in 1944. He attended the University of Saskatchewan, and S.U.N.Y. Rochester. After completing a dissertation on the Black Mountain poets, Cooley moved to Winnipeg and continues to teach Canadian and American literature and Literary Theory at St. John's College, University of Manitoba. He helped to start the Manitoba Writers Guild, and was a founding member of Turnstone Press.

Cooley is also a regular contributor to *Border Crossings*, and an editor and anthologizer of prairie writing and criticism. A few of his published books include *Bloody Jack, Perishable Light* and *Sunfall: new and selected poems*.

Robert Kroetech

is a novelist, poet and essayist. He was born in Alberta in 1927. He attended the University of Alberta and the University of Iowa, then taught at the State University of New York in Binghamton for seventeen years before moving to the University of Manitoba. His nine novels include *Badlands, What the Crow Said*, and *The Studhorse Man*, which won the Governor General's Award for Fiction for 1969. His poetry includes *Completed Field Notes* and most recently *The Hornbooks of Rita K*, which was nominated for the Governor General's Award for Poetry in 2001.

Dawne McCance

teaches theory at the University of Manitoba and edits the literary journal *Mosaic*. She reads a lot of poetry and has published a few poems and the chapbook *etymologies of dawne*.

Jon Paul Fiorentino

is the author of *Resume Drowning* (Broken Jaw Press) and *transcona fragments* (Cyclops Press/Signature Editions). His current poetry project is entitled *Hello Serotonin* and current editorial project is the anthology *Post-Prairie*—a collaborative effort with Robert Kroetsch. He is a contributing editor for *Matrix* magazine in Montreal.

Sources

Catherine Hunter
page 5 —*Latent Heat* (Winnipeg: Nuage Editions, 1997): unpaginated.
page 6 —*Latent Heat*: unpaginated
page 7 —*Latent Heat*: unpaginated
page 7 —*Latent Heat*: unpaginated
page 9 —*Lunar Wake* (Winnipeg: Turnstone Press, 1994): 35.
page 11 —*Lunar Wake*: 3.
page 13 —*Latent Heat*: unpaginated

Melanie Cameron
page 21 —*Holding the Dark* (Winnipeg: The Muses' Company, 1999): 12.
page 22 —*Holding the Dark*: 25.
page 22 —*Holding the Dark*: 67.
page 24 —*Holding the Dark*: 17.
page 27 —*Holding the Dark*: 41.
page 29 —*Holding the Dark*:107.
page 31 —*Holding the Dark*: 55.
page 33 —*Holding the Dark*: 54.

George Amabile
page 49 —Jean Baudrillard, *Simulations*. (New York: Semiotext[e], 1983): 2.

Patrick Friesen
page 68 —*The Essential Haiku, Versions of Basho, Buson, & Issa*. Ed.
    Robert Hass (Hopewell, New Jersey: Ecco Press, 1994): 11.

Méira Cook
page 77 —Carol Shields, *Various Miracles* (New York: Penguin, 1989): 61.
page 80 —Jacques Lacan, *Ecrits*. Trans. Alan Sheridan (New York: W.W.
　　　　　Norton, 1977): 157.
page 82 —Catherine Hunter, *Latent Heat* (Winnipeg: Nuage Editions,
　　　　　1997): unpaginated.
page 82 —Rob Budde, *traffick* (Winnipeg: Turnstone Press, 1999): 40.

Todd Bruce
page 85 —*Jiggers* (Winnipeg: Turnstone Press, 1993): 58.
page 86 —*Birdman* (Winnipeg: Dog Ear Press, 1992): unpaginated.
page 87 —*Jiggers*: 6.
page 89 —Julia Kristeva, *Revolution in Poetic Language*. Trans. Margaret
　　　　　Walker (New York: Columbia University Press, 1984): 79.
page 89 —*Jiggers:* 3.
page 90 —*Revolution in Poetic Language*: 206.
page 91 —*Birdman*: unpaginated.
page 91 —Elizabeth Smart, *By Grand Central Station I Sat Down and
　　　　　Wept* (Toronto: Paladin, 1966): 17.
page 92 —*Jiggers*: 53.
page 95 —*Jiggers*: 64.
page 97 —*Revolution in Poetic Language*: 16.
page 98 —*Revolution in Poetic Language*: 87.
page 99 —*Jiggers:* 66.
page 99 —*Rhapsody in D* (Winnipeg: Turnstone Press, 1997): 53.
page 99 —*Rhapsody in D*: 77.
page 100 —*Rhapsody in D*: 57.
page 100 —*Jiggers*: 22.
page 100 —*Rhapsody in D*: 45.
page 101 —*Rhapsody in D*: 53.
page 101 —*Rhapsody in D*: 3.

Dennis Cooley
page 113 —*Bloody Jack* (Winnipeg: Turnstone Press, 1984): 125.
page 113 —*Bloody Jack*: 126-127.
page 118 —*Dedication* (Saskatoon: Thistledown Press, 1988): 36.
page 119 —*Sunfall* (Concord: House of Anansi Press, 1996): 158.

Robert Kroetsch and Dawne McCance

page 123 —*Collected Field Notes* (Toronto: McClelland & Stewart, 1989): 138.

page 124 —*The Hornbooks of Rita K.* (Edmonton: University of Alberta Press, 2001): 8.

page 124 —*A Likely Story* (Red Deer: Red Deer College Press, 1995): 171-172.

page 125 —*Collected Field Notes*: 267.

page 125 —*Collected Field Notes*: 164.

page 126 —*The Hornbooks of Rita K.*: 22.

page 126 —*A Likely Story*: 187.

page 127 —*Revisions of Letters Already Sent* (Calgary: disOrientation , 1992): unpaginated.

page 128 —Mikhail Bakhtin, *Rabelais and His World*. Trans. Helene Iswolsky (Bloomington: Indiana University Press, 1984): 25.

page 131 —*etymologies of dawne* (Winnipeg: Pachyderm Press, 200): unpaginated.

page 131 —*The Hornbooks of Rita K.*: 25.

page 131 — *etymologies of dawne*: unpaginated.

page 131 — *etymologies of dawne*: unpaginated.

page 131 — *etymologies of dawne*: unpaginated.

page 133 —*Bloody Jack*: 93.

page 133 —*Seed Catalogue* (Winnipeg: Turnstone, 1986): 12.

page 134 —*Collected Field Notes*: 263.

page 135 —*Collected Field Notes*: 231.

Jon Paul Fiorentino

page 140 —*resume drowning* (Fredericton: Cauldron/Broken Jaw Press, 2002): 40.

page 141 —*transcona fragments* (Winnipeg: Cyclops Press, 2002): 94.

page 143 —*resume drowning*: 56.